Fired, Laid-Off or Forced Out

A Complete Guide to Severance, Benefits and Your Rights When You're Starting Over

Richard C. Busse
Attorney at Law

SPHINX® PUBLISHING
AN IMPRINT OF SOURCEBOOKS, INC.®
NAPERVILLE, ILLINOIS
www.SphinxLegal.com

First Edition: 2005

Published by: **Sphinx® Publishing, An Imprint of Sourcebooks, Inc.®**

<u>Naperville Office</u>
P.O. Box 4410
Naperville, Illinois 60567-4410
630-961-3900
Fax: 630-961-2168
www.sourcebooks.com
www.SphinxLegal.com/Sphinx

This publication is designed to provide accurate and authoritative information in regard to the subject matter covered. It is sold with the understanding that the publisher is not engaged in rendering legal, accounting, or other professional service. If legal advice or other expert assistance is required, the services of a competent professional person should be sought.

From a Declaration of Principles Jointly Adopted by a Committee of the American Bar Association and a Committee of Publishers and Associations

This product is not a substitute for legal advice.

Disclaimer required by Texas statutes.

Library of Congress Cataloging-in-Publication Data
Busse, Richard C.
  Fired, laid off or forced out : a complete guide to severance, benefits and your rights when you're starting over / by Richard C. Busse.-- 1st ed.
    p. cm.
  Includes index.
  ISBN 1-57248-459-4 (pbk. : alk. paper)
  1. Employees--Dismissal of--United States. 2. Unemployment--United States. 3. Psychology, Industrial. I. Title.

HF5549.5.D55B87 2005
650.1--dc22
                                                                2005025685

Printed and bound in the United States of America.

BG — 10 9 8 7 6 5 4 3 2 1

ACKNOWLEDGMENT

I would like to thank my editors, Dianne Wheeler and Michael Bowen; my paralegal, Shirley Rayner, for her careful assistance; the entire staff at Sourcebooks for their wonderful support; my family for their inspiration; and particularly my mother, W. Kay Busse, for leading the way.

Contents

The Exit Interview
Your Final Check and Benefits
Posttermination Filings to Protect Your Rights
The Effect of Termination on Your Receipt of Benefits
Termination Tips
Termination Tips

Chapter 8: Immediately after Your Termination 77

Remain Calm
Ask Probing Questions
Remove All Personal Belongings at Your Earliest Opportunity
Relinquish All Keys and ID Badges when Requested
Record What was Said in the Termination Meeting
Request a Copy of Your Personnel File
Let Your Family and Friends Take Care of You
If You Need It, Seek Emotional Counseling
Seek Legal Advice Only from a Knowledgeable Lawyer
As Soon as You are Able, Look for Other Work
Do Not Start Cutting Your Own Deal
Do Not Release Your Employer Without Consulting a Lawyer
Do Not Write a Letter of Protest to the Company
Do Not Start Writing Letters to Your Congressional Delegation
Do Not Engage in Physical Harm
Do Not Remove Anything that Does Not Belong to You
Do Not Refuse to Return Property Belonging to the Employer
Do Not Immediately File an Internal, Nonunion Grievance
Do Not Sign a Confession
Do Not Try to Handle it Alone
Termination Tips

Chapter 9: Negotiating a Severance Agreement 87

How to Get More Severance
The Contents of Your Severance Agreement
Severance Tips List

Chapter 10: All About Lawyers 97

How to Find a Lawyer
Engaging Your Lawyer

Introduction

This book is intended for those who fear they are about to be or who have been terminated. It is written to teach survival skills to keep someone from becoming a candidate for termination. In it, I have sought to impart all of the experience I have gained from thirty years' practice in the field of employment law.

As you will discover in this book, most people who have been terminated cannot bring a lawsuit against their former employer. Most employees are *at-will* employees—meaning that they can be terminated for any reason or no reason at all, unless the termination falls within one of the few exceptions to that general rule.

This book first discusses what those exceptions are and briefly reviews unlawful termination law. Then it explores strategies to minimize the risk of being terminated. For those who cannot avoid a termination, the steps to follow if it occurs are discussed. Finally, it takes an in-depth look at employment law and goes through the litigation process, from choosing a lawyer to settling the case.

This book is not intended to be, nor is it a substitute for, legal advice. To the extent federal laws, legal principles, state laws, or the holding of cases are cited, they are all subject to change. They also may not apply because the facts of each particular case or the laws of each state may be different.

To the extent the book contains observations about the dynamics of the workplace and strategies for survival in it, they are necessarily stated in generalities. Within each state, widely varying degrees of compliance with laws by companies exist. In any given city, there may be both progressive and reactionary employers, enlightened or *old school* CEO's, and strong or weak human resource managers. Some of the strategies mentioned here will work with some managers, but may not with others. They are intended to be helpful guidelines to stimulate thought about ways in which you might be able to help yourself. Modify them with the help of an experienced employment attorney to fit your style and your situation.

This book is not intended to be a complete survey of employment law. (For example, it does not discuss wage and hour law.) Its focus is on the problems facing the terminated or soon-to-be terminated worker. For a primer on employment law, I refer you to my book *Employees' Rights: Your Practical Handbook To Workplace Law,* Sphinx Publishing (2004).

Chapter 1

Discharge as an At-Will Employee

For most of us, any termination is shocking. For some, it is even debilitating. For others, it ruins their careers, if not their health. A termination, and the loss of income that accompanies its aftermath, can divide families and destroy the soul. It can cause shame, humiliation, and embarrassment to the terminated worker who realizes that his or her children will not have anything for Christmas this year or cannot attend that special school. It can destroy the psyche and cause a loss of self-esteem that takes years to rebuild. A termination always has the potential to be a life-altering event.

Why is the unplanned loss of a job so momentous? Most of us have to engage in some kind of work during the great bulk of our adult life. That means that for most of us, our most important asset is our own *marketability* as a worker. That marketability can be substantially impaired if we are fired. All of us have only one work history.

Typically, employers will ask applicants to complete an application for employment by including their work history for the last five- to fifteen-year period. It is not unusual for a résumé to include one's entire work history. In applications for employment, the dates of employment and reason for leaving former employers are typically requested. If you do not honestly report the reason for leaving, it is grounds for termination from your prospective employment. If you do honestly report in the application that you have a termination on your record, it will at least require explanation, and you may lose the job prospect on that account. A termination is not only traumatic, it also creates a lingering stain on your permanent employment record that you will have to carry with you for the rest of your working life.

Until recently, most employees injured by a termination could do nothing about it. Unless you are a union worker or in a civil service position that can only be terminated *for cause*, in all likelihood you are an *at-will employee*. Simply stated, at-will employment means that the employee works *at the pleasure of the employer* for no definite term and can be terminated for any lawful reason (or for no reason at all). The at-will employment rule still prevails in every state except Montana—the only state in which *universal for cause protection* is mandated by state statute for all employees who have passed their probationary period.

The development of employee rights in the last forty years has dramatically altered the balance of power between employees and employers. Although employers are still largely free to discriminate and harass employees, great inroads have been made to bar their power to do so. Many exceptions to the employment at will rule have been overwhelmingly adopted to prevent a termination from occurring with impunity if based on *protected class status* or *protected activity*. In most states, additional remedies for wrongful discharge or breach of contract may be pursued.

Where it is recognized, a remedy for wrongful discharge is allowed only when the termination is contrary to *public policy*. Generally, a discharge will be held to be contrary to public policy if it was committed because the employee had engaged in some kind of activity the law must protect or else the intent of the law will be frustrated. Apart from the law of wrongful discharge, a termination can be unlawful if it violates a law passed by Congress or a state legislature, such as a discrimination, retaliation, or *whistleblowing* statute. In addition, a termination can also be unlawful if it violates an enforceable promise made by the employer. Because employment law is so commonly misunderstood, it is useful to first put away the frequently heard myths about employment rights.

Debunking Myths about Your Employment Rights

As stated, most employees are at-will employees who may be terminated for any or no reason, unless the real reason falls within one of the exceptions to that rule. Because those exceptions are not well understood and may not apply in some situations, employees are frequently misinformed about the extent of their legal protection at the very time it matters most—when they must respond to an adverse personnel action.

What follows are the top ten *incorrect* notions held by employees about their employment rights.

1. There is due process in the workplace.

Most workers can be terminated at the whim of the employer at any time, for any lawful reason, with or without due process. Even employers who purport to follow a *progressive discipline* system, in which progressively severe levels of discipline will precede termination, typically retain the right to skip steps and proceed to termination immediately. There are only four exceptions to the general no due process rule that are only available to limited groups of workers. Those exceptions are:

+ union workers with a strong collective bargaining agreement;
+ non-management government workers in the public sector;
+ Nevada workers in cases when an employee's integrity is questioned on information by a *spotter*; and,
+ workers with an employment contract specifically granting due process.

2. You have a right to know why you have been terminated.

Except in Indiana, Maine, Minnesota, and Missouri—where an employer must provide a written statement of reasons for termination to a terminated employee—your employer does not have to tell you why you were fired. In the great majority of states, your employer can simply tell you, "You're fired." While that may create anger and only drive you to seek out a lawyer, in forty-six states, that is the only information your employer is required to give you.

3. If you are hired for a particular job, your employer cannot change it.

Except for restrictions contained in collective bargaining agreements, self-imposed government regulations, or individual employment contracts, although you may have been recruited or hired for one position, your employer can change your job altogether after you are hired. You are free to refuse to accept the change, but if you do, your employer is likewise free to fire you for your refusal.

4. After you are hired, your employer cannot reduce your pay.

Subject to contract requirements and government regulations, an employer is free to reduce your pay prospectively. Although an employer cannot hire you today for $10.00 an hour and pay you $8.00 at the end of the day, it can tell you today that if you show up for work tomorrow, your pay will be $8.00 from that point forward.

5. You have free speech rights to express your opinion at work.

The guarantee of free speech that is contained in the Bill of Rights to the United States Constitution is a limitation on governmental power, not the power of private individuals or entities (such as corporations). Therefore, an employer is free to terminate you for expressing your opinion. (The exception is in Connecticut, which by statute prohibits both public and private employers from, in some circumstances, terminating employees for speaking out on matters of public concern.)

6. On-the-job harassment is illegal.

There is no law against harassment, generally. While some employers may prohibit harassment in the form of an enforceable policy statement, harassment itself becomes illegal only if it was committed because of your *protected class status*. So unless you are being harassed because of your race, color, sex, age, religion, or disability, or because you have engaged in *protected activity* (such as resisting sexual harassment), nothing bars an employer from engaging in some form of harassing behavior toward you.

7. On-the-job discrimination is illegal.

Discrimination, like harassment, is not unlawful, generally. An employer is free to discriminate by giving better treatment to some employees over others (as long as it is not because of an employee's membership in a protected class or because they had engaged in some form of protected activity).

8. Your boss cannot retaliate against you.

Retaliation, in general, is not unlawful. Retaliation becomes unlawful when it is committed because an employee has engaged in activity that is protected as a matter of public policy, such as reporting illegal activity, reporting to jury duty, filing a workers' compensation claim, or resisting sexual harassment.

In addition, retaliation can be unlawful if your employer has entered into a binding agreement not to retaliate against you if, for example, you utilize its open door policy. Most employers, however, try not to make unqualified legally enforceable promises like that to their employees.

9. Your boss must be fair with you.

There is no law that expressly says an employer must be *fair* with you. Therefore, with few exceptions, there is no law requiring your employer to be fair with you in making employment decisions that affect you.

10. Your employer must always choose the best qualified person.

There is no law that expressly requires an employer to hire the best qualified candidate for a position. Outside of some civil service constraints in the public sector, such as qualification lists for police and fire positions, there is no law barring employers from hiring unqualified candidates. (This may not be the wisest business decision, but it occurs frequently—think family members.)

Chapter 2

Strategies to Survive a Disciplinary Action

If you are reading this because you fear a termination is in your future, you may now learn how to avoid it altogether. Not every rocky employment situation will inevitably result in termination. Sometimes, all that is required is the exercise of care and good judgment to reestablish a healthy working relationship with your boss. In other cases, it is more difficult to find common ground. Therefore, before assuming that a termination is inevitable, explore some strategies to survive a threatened termination and extend your employment.

Are You Really on a Termination Track?

To employers, unnecessary employee turnover is expensive. It is costly to train new employees and to dispose of experienced workers who are generally more productive. If an employee can be saved from termination through a disciplinary process designed to give notice of perceived deficiencies with a fair opportunity to correct those deficiencies—productivity is saved and those costs are avoided.

Most employers follow a pattern in their disciplinary practices, which are typically embodied in written policies. Usually, disciplinary policies incorporate (in some fashion) the concept of *progressive discipline*, whereby employees are given progressively severe stages of discipline if they do not respond. Most follow a pattern whereby a *verbal warning* is to be followed by at least one *written warning* before termination. However, you should not assume you have been given a verbal warning merely because your employer speaks with you about improving your performance. In most cases, your supervisor will consider that *coaching* or *counseling*, is something completely outside the disciplinary process.

If a disciplinary track has begun in your case, it does not mean you are destined for termination, regardless of what you may think of your supervisor's hostility towards you. However, as disturbing as it may be to you to have received what may be the first disciplinary action in the whole work history, a demonstration of compliance with that warning might correct the problem. Do not automatically assume that you are destined for termination simply because you have received employee discipline. Otherwise, you may overreact and create an even greater problem.

How Employee Discipline Works

Just because an employer has a progressive disciplinary system does not mean that the employer will follow it. Typically, disciplinary systems are communicated to workers in employee handbooks. Although promises in handbooks can become an enforceable contract between an employer and its employees—in most cases they will not. Employers pay lawyers to write those handbooks and include within them special clauses, known as *disclaimers*, to render meaningless any apparent language of a binding promise contained in the handbook. A typical disclaimer may look like what follows.

Nothing herein shall be construed to constitute a contract of employment. You are an employee at will who can be terminated at any time for any or no reason. Management retains the right at any time to deviate from or change the policies contained herein.

Most courts give effect to disclaimers like that. As a result, if an employer deviates from the explanation of the process it says it will follow in the handbook, most courts will not allow employees to sue for breach of contract if such a disclaimer exists. Sometimes an employee can get around the disclaimer in situations when it is not sufficiently prominent to give the employee fair notice. Some courts have also refused to automatically enforce disclaimers when the language of the disclaimer is inconsistent with provisions contained elsewhere in the handbook, making the inconsistency a question the jury must decide. These are still rare exceptions that do not often trump the general disclaimer rules.

Regardless of whether an employer is legally obligated to adhere to its disciplinary system, they generally train managers to follow whatever disciplinary system is in place. They do so to encourage consistency in the application of their work rules, partly to avoid the creation of legal liability. An employer may not be liable to an employee for breach of contract in failing to adhere to its disciplinary system because of the existence of effective disclaimers. However, its failure to do so may serve as evidence of intent in a wrongful discharge or discrimination case. Many cases hold that a deviation from a company's stated personnel policy raises an inference of discrimination.

For example, a rogue manager—who has an ax to grind with a worker who reported that manager for sexual harassment—may put that worker on a disciplinary *fast track*. Fully aware of that tendency, employers charge human resources departments with the responsibility of ensuring that their procedures are consistently applied. To that end, many employers will go so far as to require human resources' approval before a worker can be fired.

How to Survive Employee Discipline

Most terminations are avoidable. In most cases, employees are asked to adhere to performance standards that are well within their ability to conform. The greater danger to an employee's employment security usually relates to the employee's reaction to the discipline that has been imposed. There are things you can do to survive pending discipline and minimize the risk of making the situation worse.

SURVIVING PENDING DISCIPLINE, GENERALLY

One thing within your control in your effort to survive pending discipline is to respond positively and constructively. You may disagree with your supervisor that the discipline was merited. However, your supervisor is the boss—not you. If the matter becomes a struggle over who is in charge, you will lose that battle every time. By the same token, it is frequently the case that conflicts that rise to the level of formal discipline are precisely that—a struggle for authority. Your supervisor may sense that you do not respect him or her, or he or she may be threatened by you because you are smarter, more experienced, or have greater support amongst your peers. However, for your part, you may be vocal, argumentative, or simply unskilled in verbal communications, and come off sounding like a smart alec.

Instead of arguing with your supervisor about the wisdom or fairness of giving you discipline, simply accept the discipline and demonstrate your willingness to subordinate yourself to your supervisor's authority. You may be surprised by how easily you can diffuse this potentially volatile situation with this simple act. In the vast majority of cases, once an employee does that, the supervisor will relent.

The most unpleasant part of any supervisor's job is to manage the personnel problems that come with it. If a supervisor can avoid having to spend an inordinate amount of time dealing with an employee under formal discipline, he or she usually will.

SURVIVING VERBAL WARNINGS

If you have been unable to avoid the first step in the disciplinary process—typically a verbal warning—you should try to immediately correct the objective behavior that is to account for the warning. For example, if tardiness is the problem, you must take extraordinary care not to repeat the offense. If you are an employee at will, it does not matter that you were late to work for a reason beyond your control, such as from a freeway tie-up or an alarm that did not go off. You will be held responsible for being at work on time, regardless of whether you are at fault.

On the other hand, if a health problem is to account for the tardiness, it is your responsibility to supply your employer with sufficient information so it views this not as a problem with your behavior, but as a problem with your health. Further, your employer cannot be expected to rely on *your* medical opinion. Under the *Americans with Disabilities Act* (ADA), if you have a disability, you may be entitled to a *reasonable accommodation*. Under the ADA, it may be legally sufficient for you to put your employer on notice of a need for accommodation by just telling your employer that you have a medical concern. In order to get your employer to fully cooperate, however, you may need to present your employer with a note from your doctor. This note should inform your employer of your diagnosis, tell your employer that you are under medical treatment for the condition, and request some kind of reasonable accommodation.

If a verbal warning is more subjective in nature—a *poor attitude*, for example—your task is more difficult. Again, such warnings are usually related to the employee's refusal to show the supervisor the respect the supervisor believes he or she deserves. Therefore, you may need to show your supervisor respect even when you do not actually respect your supervisor. Show that respect in both your verbal and nonverbal communications. Having to demonstrate the required level of respect, even when it is not deserved, is not always as humiliating as it sounds. You can show respect by keeping disrespectful opinions to yourself when speaking to your supervisor, particularly in front of others. Even well-meant suggestions, if presented in the wrong way, can be construed by your supervisor to be quarrelsome behavior.

Further, if your supervisor believes you have a tendency to engage in such behavior, he or she will assume you are generally that way, and you will have to take care that your nonverbal communication is not misconstrued to be equally offensive. A disgusted facial expression, a heavy sigh of frustration, or crossed arms and a defensive stare can challenge your supervisor. If you engage in such behavior in the presence of your supervisor, even unintentionally or for unrelated reasons, you may bait your supervisor into calling you out to say what you really think. This may force you into a situation that you do not want to be in.

If changing your attitude is difficult or you are a transparent person and find it difficult to hide your true feelings, it may be useful for you to look to a peer in the workplace whom you trust for advice, and ask that person to coach you. He or she can help you determine whether and how you are displaying disrespect. Then, as you internalize whatever advice your coach gives, you may wish to use him or her to ensure that you continue to effectively change the way you present yourself to your supervisor in the workplace.

If you disrespect your supervisor to others behind his or her back, it will be even harder not to display that disrespect in their presence. Indeed, the source of the problem may be that your supervisor may have heard that you were *bad-mouthing* him or her to others. Once that stops outside your supervisor's presence, your supervisor will know it. It will then be easier for you to display respect to your supervisor in person in front of your co-workers when you no longer feel you have to keep up appearances.

Initially, check in with your coach two or three times a day, for a week or so. Then check in daily for two to three weeks, or until the two of you are satisfied that if there is a problem, the problem is not you. Make sure that both you and your coach keep what you are doing confidential. An employer does not appreciate someone stirring up trouble by broadcasting that they think they are being unfairly disciplined.

SURVIVING WRITTEN WARNINGS

If you have been unable to stem the tide and your supervisor steps it up to the next higher disciplinary level and issues you a written warning, do not react in anger. Whatever you do under the influence of anger will probably be wrong and damaging to your career. Again, particularly in cases of persons with long, distinguished careers, the problem may not be one of performance. It is not uncommon that a supervisor, particularly a new one, feels threatened by a subordinate's superior expertise. In other cases, the supervisor may feel that the subordinate is resistant to change and stubbornly insistent on clinging to the *old ways* of doing things, even though your performance level may be the same as what the supervisor finds acceptable in others. If you become incensed and challenge your supervisor for having the nerve to discipline you, that will only tend to make your supervisor think he or she cannot work with you. Therefore, do not react immediately. Take time to reflect before you react.

That does not mean that you cannot say anything about the receipt of a written warning. Typically, a written warning will be given to you in person. The supervisor will often be accompanied by someone from human resources. If you are a union member, you may be accompanied by your shop steward. At the meeting, you may be told verbally why you are getting the written warning. In other cases, you may simply be told to read it or it may be read to you. In any event, try to not be argumentative. Stay focused on what you are hearing. You cannot stay focused if you become too agitated. Try to remain calm and listen carefully. That way, when you are asked if you understood what was just told or read to you, you will be in a position to affirmatively respond and to gather information if necessary. You will also be in a better position to accurately record what happened later on.

If necessary, seek clarification without being argumentative. Not all managers or people in human resources are clear in their communications. The written warning may not be clear in its identification of the incident on which it is based. The warning may refer to a work operation you frequently perform, and in order to get a fix on the incident referred to, you will need to ask when the offense supposedly occurred. You may need to seek clarification about what precisely you are alleged to have done. This may be particularly necessary if no one spoke with you to get your side of the story when the incident occurred before concluding that you were guilty of the offense.

If you have information about the merits of the charge, you can ask permission to say something in your defense. Rarely, though, will whatever you say make any difference. Still, if the warning is predicated on misinformation, you need to say so right then. Otherwise, your silence may be misconstrued as a tacit admission and any later explanation may be viewed by the employer with suspicion. In most cases, however, you will simply want to have your supervisor explain what he or she thinks you did wrong and tell you what they think you need to do to correct the problem.

SURVIVING PERFORMANCE IMPROVEMENT PLANS

The written warning may take the form of a letter, or it may be presented alongside or as part of what is sometimes called a *plan of assistance* or *performance improvement plan*. Most often, such plans are instituted after a poor annual performance appraisal, but they can follow, or become a part of, a written warning. Typically, under such plans, you are told that your performance must improve to a certain level within a specified period of time or else you will be terminated.

Human resource managers are taught (and teach managers) that in developing such plans, the performance goals of the plan are to be realistic and ascertainable. In setting those goals, they are to interject as much objectivity as possible, so that the employee will be able to know—without guesswork—what the employer will deem to be successful performance. Typically, the performance goals that are set for the employee in the plan must be met within a given time frame. Again, in principle, that time frame is also to be realistic.

If the goals of the written warning or plan of assistance are too subjective, so that you cannot be sure how your performance will be measured or what level of performance is expected, you can try to negotiate clearer standards. Apart from negotiating clearer goals, it may be that there are particular obstacles to meeting stated goals, which should be taken into account in fixing the required level of performance. For example, you may be asked to adhere to a particular production requirement on a printing press, but with some printing jobs you cannot adhere to the requirement. It may be that a big, slow job is about to start. Whatever the special problem, if it exists, it should be mentioned in your effort to negotiate a fair set of goals.

On the other hand, do not contentiously argue that your supervisor's plan is too vague, if in fact it is reasonably clear. If you demand that your supervisor state more precisely what it is you are expected to do, he or she will—and you will regret having made the point.

Once you commence your performance during the plan, you may be required to meet with your supervisor periodically to update your performance. Let your supervisor take the lead. If your supervisor misses a meeting, it is usually best not to insist on having one—unless your plan specifically states it is your responsibility to see that the planned meetings take place. This is quite rare. That may be a sign that your supervisor is losing interest in *riding herd* on you. Allow the issues your supervisor has with you to take lower priority on their list of things to do. Likewise, do not remind your supervisor that you are a problem employee by continually asking "How am I doing?" Just tend to your own performance. If planned meetings occur, use them as an opportunity to leave the impression that you are a team player who is willing to support management, and more importantly, your immediate supervisor.

If issues come up during the performance period under the plan that call for clarification from your supervisor, freely seek it. If you have any doubt your supervisor will recall the instructions or stand by them, memorialize the clarifying instructions you are given in a respectful memo or email.

At the end of the performance period, you will be wondering what comes next. You will have the natural urge to seek reassurance that your employer is not planning on firing you. You must resist that urge. If you go to your employer and ask, "Are you going to fire me," it will only remind your supervisor that he or she can. Believe it or not, in most cases, your supervisor will have more pressing issues than *you* to think of. Your goal is to allow those other pressing issues to be the focus of your supervisor's attention—not you.

SURVIVING SUSPENSIONS AND INVOLUNTARY LEAVES

The most serious discipline—short of termination—is a *suspension*. Most employers do not suspend for performance deficiencies after a written warning—they just terminate. However, some employers feel that for some offenses, such as excessive absenteeism, it does not hurt to give an otherwise productive employee one last chance to change his or her behavior. If you are placed on suspension, once you return you are bound to strictly comply with the rules, or else you will be fired. The exception would be if your employer takes the position that any further offense is too trivial, dissimilar, or remote in time to justify a termination.

The most frequent question that arises in the case of suspensions relates to the passage of time. What if you return and your performance is perfect for the rest of that year and the better part of the next year? At what point does the suspension become so old or stale that it is unreasonable for your employer to just terminate you for a repetition of that offense, without going back through all the disciplinary steps again? There are no fixed rules about this issue. If you are an employee at will, no noncontractual obligation will require your employer to start over, unless you can prove that its failure to do so is motivated by your protected class status or protected activity. However, the longer the period between the suspension and the termination, the easier that will be to prove.

An involuntary leave—with or without pay—may be used by an employer when an employee is charged with serious misconduct. This will get the employee out of the workplace pending the results of an investigation. Employees can be placed on leave with or without previous discipline. Those charged with sexual harassment, suspected of theft or embezzlement, or who are first-line supervisors charged with abusive conduct of their peers are often sent home, typically with pay, while the investigation proceeds. At any time the leave may be converted to an unpaid leave. This often occurs when the employee who is sent home either fails to cooperate with the investigation, abandons employment, or is believed by the employer to be guilty of the offense.

One problem that sometimes occurs when an employer allows the leave to go on too long occurs if the suspended employee is a manager. Each day a manager is out of the workplace, his or her authority erodes. Sometimes a lawyer's help is required in such cases to gently motivate the employer to expeditiously conclude the investigation, and if no grounds exist for termination, to restore the employee to his or her rightful position.

If you are suspended, the thing to remember is that you are still an employee of the company, even if you are suspended without pay. If you care to maintain your employment relationship during a suspension, you must take care to follow whatever directions given by your employer. Your employer may have a call-in requirement or may require you to be at home during certain times of the day.

Your employer may require you to participate in any investigation. Your obligation to cooperate with your employer during an investigation continues during the suspension period. If you do not cooperate and follow the instructions you are given, it could be taken as job abandonment, or could constitute a final offense that merits termination. If you have a good wrongful discharge case developing, you do not want to spoil it by engaging in conduct that seemingly breaks the causal connection between your protected activity or class status and the impending termination.

DEALING WITH THE AFTERMATH

Once you survive the formal warning or suspension period, there will be the aftermath to deal with. The discipline will remain a part of your personnel file. If there is a recurrence of the offense, more serious discipline could follow. That history may influence your next performance review, scheduled raise, and whether you get a promotion. But first you have a relationship you need to deal with—the one with your boss.

To cause a reduction in hostilities, you need to mend that relationship as soon as possible. Most bosses feel it is the employee's responsibility, not theirs. You will need to take the initiative in putting closure on this episode. You will need to show the supervisor that you will still be supportive and that there are no hard feelings.

One way to start mending the relationship is to employ the *three contact rule*. Pick out three reasons to ask your supervisor's advice about something once each week for three successive weeks. Select subjects that are safe, so that you will be prepared to follow whatever advice your supervisor gives. Approach your supervisor and ask his or her opinion about that subject. Appear interested in his or her opinion and receptive to his or her advice. Let you supervisor know later that you followed his or her advice and thank him or her for it. The object of the exercise is that by the end of the third contact, as you are walking away, your supervisor will think, *I can work with this person.*

Still, there are some supervisors who rule by fear and intimidation and who would never be happy about anyone questioning them about anything. If that is your type of supervisor, you should show respect by simply staying away and keeping your head down.

Top Ten Rules to Survive Discipline

Whether you are on a termination track or not, your own actions play a large part in your ultimate survival. Do not behave in a defensive manner if you are verbally counseled so as not to motivate your supervisor to move to formal discipline. If you are given formal discipline, do not overreact. That may only give your supervisor reason to step up the disciplinary process to show you who is boss. Follow the Top Ten Rules to Survive Discipline to maximize the odds your employer will back off and give itself credit for *saving* you from termination.

Top Ten Rules to Survive Discipline

1. Do not make it about a struggle over who is boss.
2. Demonstrate your willingness to comply.
3. Consider using a coach to ensure that you are not acting disrespectfully.
4. If your supervisor gives you further discipline, do not react in anger.
5. Respectfully try to clarify what is expected.
6. Do not keep asking, "How am I doing?"
7. Do not insist that your boss keep the scheduled one-on-one meetings with you.
8. Clarify any vague instructions, and document your performance and any requests for support.
9. Never ask, "Am I going to be fired?"
10. Use the three contact rule to put closure on the crisis period.

Chapter 3

How to Diffuse Potentially Volatile Situations

As only a small number of firings are unlawful, the odds are that yours will not be unlawful. Therefore, because you may not be able to sue if you are fired, or if it may not be in your best interest to do so even if you are able, you must utilize all your personal skills to do what you can to avoid a termination from happening. The strategies available to employees to accomplish this are somewhat dependent upon their position in an organization.

Strategies for Executives

For the CEO, executive director of a nonprofit organization, or city manager, there are strategies you can follow to reduce tension and volatility in the workplace. In fact, since most entities are typically less hampered by process in terminating their highest ranking executive officers, more strategies are open to you than others, either to retain your position or to negotiate a favorable severance package. Executives in the public sector have broader options than those in the private sector, because the elected board or council to which they report is seldom handpicked by the board chair. Strategies may be more limited for the executive in the private sector, where it is much more common—particularly in a closely held corporation—for board members to be personally selected by and beholden to the board chair.

Strategies for the Chief Executive Officer of a Government Body

Elected officials and their personal staff, who usually consist of political supporters and campaign workers, have job security during the term of office of the successful candidate. However, the chief executive officer of a local government body—whether that position is called city manager, county manager, executive director, or CAO—is much less secure. Indeed, candidates for elective local office may have run on a platform to oust that person. Because of constitutional protections associated with free speech, the persons occupying executive positions with government bodies are usually sitting on a tinderbox. At any moment, controversial issues may make continued employment practically unbearable. Yet, people of all levels of talent have historically answered their calling to such positions and typically wish to retain them if they can.

In contrast with the private sector, in which employment agreements often govern the rights of the parties in any impending separation, public entities less often use such agreements. Therefore, relationships—not documents—provide the public sector chief executive with the greatest potential for leverage.

Should you, as a public sector CEO, be faced with the threat of termination, the first thing you should do is assess the strength of the threat. It is not unusual for a city manager, for example, to always have one detractor on the city council. Typically, little danger of termination looms under those circumstances. Your priority in that case is to appease the detractor and to take special care to appease any likely allies of the detractor. This will help discourage the formation of an effective coalition spearheaded by the detractor.

Should you believe that such a coalition is in the process of forming, you should assess whether it would be more advantageous to intervene and prevent its formation (and risk a backlash) or to abide its formation and take its measure afterward. That determination will often depend upon the apparent strength or weakness of the prospective coalition. The weaker the coalition, whether in numbers or influence, the less active intervention is indicated. Any intervention carries with it the potential for a backlash, by generating additional support for the coalition by board members not otherwise predisposed to join.

Boards and board members view themselves—perhaps rightfully—as all-powerful, and any effort by a nonelected official to assault the prerogatives of one board member is often viewed by the others as an assault on them all. They think, *if the city manager can do that to Commissioner Smith, it could happen to me, too.* Therefore, if the presumed coalition is made up of those who are not the strongest board members (and perhaps even includes those who are considered to be fringe element board members, as is sometimes the case), let that coalition happen and avoid the risk of active intervention.

On the other hand, if the prospective coalition threatens to include a majority of the board or its most influential members, sometimes it is prudent to attempt to prevent its formation. The goal here is to prevent the making of political alliances that cannot be undone over a small matter, such as your own personal welfare. If that is your assessment, then you may have no choice but to move speedily to intervene in its formation.

How is that intervention accomplished? First, you need to assess your remaining support on the board. Count and rank your supporters according to you assessment of the strength of their allegiance. Then, approach your strongest supporter on the board and enlist his or her help in securing support from a majority of the board members. Solicit his or her ideas and carefully consider his or her input. Suggest to him or her that the two of you approach your next strongest supporter to form a coalition. Then the three of you should meet and determine which of the remaining board members to approach, in what order, and by what means. (It may be, for example, that the next most favorable board member is fairly neutral to you, but is very close to and is subject to influence by one of your other supporters.)

One by one, approach each member and obtain a commitment. Continue this process until, hopefully, a majority of the board has committed to you. Even after you have done that, however, you must consider whether to end any further board member contact and surprise the balance of the board at the next board meeting with a no vote on the motion to oust you. Another option is to attempt to hinder the attack altogether by informing the remaining uncommitted board members that they do not have the votes they need. The determination of which tactic to pursue will depend upon other considerations. These include the personality of the principal antagonist, how much he or she would want to be spared the public embarrassment of being outvoted, and the danger that advance notice will allow your antagonist the opportunity to flip a marginal supporter. That decision may be reduced to the personal charisma of the antagonist and your assessment of that person's ability to play the fringe board members.

In the public sector, the board chair's influence is often determined by that public body's form of government. If, under your employer's form of government, that person has power to assign responsibilities to other board members, the enhanced authority makes the chair more threatening. Regardless of that person's authority, however, alliances are often determined by *vote-swapping* on *pet issues*. Before casting your fate on a particular strategy, be sure you have a complete understanding of what each of your supporters on the board wants and needs, and the power of the board chair to help or hinder each from getting it.

STRATEGIES FOR THE CHIEF EXECUTIVE OFFICER OF A PRIVATE ENTITY FOR-PROFIT CORPORATION

The strategies for the CEO of a private company are fundamentally the same as for other chief executives, except in consideration of the special influences associated with a for-profit corporation. Specifically, while all board members of a private for-profit corporation have one vote, not all board members have equal influence, principally because of imbalances in stock ownership. Indeed, in some small companies where the stock is controlled by just a few persons, those owners can vote to simply remove antagonistic or uncooperative board members. In larger companies, such influence may be diluted but is practically the same, because it is difficult for minority owners to marshal enough votes to form an effective opposing block.

That inordinate influence, though, can be used to your advantage when you can argue to the majority shareholder that a personality clash between you and the board chair should take lower priority than your exemplary performance. It may be that the controlling shareholder attributes the handsome return on their investment to your efforts and would oppose any attempt by the board chair to oust you over a petty personality issue. In such cases, contact with that shareholder or board representative might be in order. It would be advisable before doing so to first enlist the support of a few supporters on the board who could join with you in that contact and vouch for your accurate characterization of the dispute as one over mere personality differences. Your ability to manage stockholder support is particularly important in tough economic times, when existing stockholders take on even more powerful profiles as they are being tapped by their corporations for additional investments.

STRATEGIES FOR THE CHIEF EXECUTIVE OFFICER OF A PRIVATE NONPROFIT CORPORATION

The strategies previously stated for other CEO's are equally applicable here. The difference in the case of private nonprofit corporations, which have no shareholders, relates to two other issues— sources of funding and the dominant personality. As for the first, it is not unusual for a nonprofit corporation to have a single benefactor who over the years has been its *white knight*. Unless you are able to secure that person's support, or at least neutralize that person's opposition, there will be little chance for your survival. The only way to survive in the face of that person's opposition would be to lessen their influence by replacing their superior funding position with other funding sources. That takes time you may not have.

The other nuance associated with nonprofit corporations has to do with the dominant personality. It is often the case that the person who founded the organization is its first CEO and only becomes board chair when he or she becomes tired of doing all the leg work. It is frequently difficult, however, for those persons to relinquish control over the day-to-day operations of the entity to others. The pride of foundership often brings that person into conflict with his or her successor, who the founder believes is taking the organization off track. If that is your case, you will lose that struggle—regardless of how excellent your leadership—unless you are able to persuade the principal funding source and many of the other board members that the board chair is out of step with changes that are required to keep the organization competitive with others fighting for the same funding dollars.

Strategies for Mid-level Managers

For the most part, mid-level managers who survive the first year or two of employment are there for the long haul. Absent economic layoffs, promotion to a position of vulnerability, or replacement of their supervisor with an antagonist, many mid-level managers stay in their positions for years. In spite of this long-term thinking, it is this middle position that makes you vulnerable if a termination is on the horizon.

You have fewer tools at your disposal with which to exert power with the organization. By definition, your power is subordinate to the manager above you. Even peak performers who deliver profits within their organization year after year may not have enough influence to thwart the will of a jealous boss to remove or demote them.

DO NOT DO ANYTHING TO LOSE SUPPORT

The most important truth to understand as a mid-level manager is that you are not all that powerful, irrespective of your performance. That realization, in turn, should cause you to understand that without the support of other higher-ups, you are just as vulnerable to removal as anyone else. Consequently, the first rule for you is that you must take care not to say or do anything that would risk losing support. That means you need to be cognizant of certain organizational imperatives, the cornerstone of which is to respect chain of command.

If you do not get along with your supervisor or disagree with the business ethics of his or her decisions, the first person to speak with about it, even if in rather oblique terms, is your supervisor. You can bet that if you go directly to your supervisor's boss instead, the first thing he or she will ask is, "Have you discussed this with your supervisor?" If you have not, do not be surprised if you are given an immediate directive to do so.

A company is built like a pyramid. Management is supremely aware that unless each rung enjoys the support of the next lower rung, the organization will collapse. If you do not respect this organizational imperative, no one will want you to work for them, because they will believe you would not be capable of supporting them either. If you go outside the organizational lines you risk making yourself a pariah.

What if you are asked to do something you believe is illegal? Ordinarily, your first move should still be to express to the person giving you that directive that you think the action is improper and state your reasons why. You should give that person an opportunity to withdraw the directive. If they do not withdraw the directive after your inquiry, consider memorializing that conversation and the exact directive that was given in a factual, nonemotional email or memo directed to him or her afterwards. You can invite him or her to let you know by email if you did not get it right. Otherwise, if you do not approach them first, but rather go first to human resources or a corporate hotline, you would leave that person free to say that what you allege was not what was said or meant at all. The corporation would then be free to say it was all a big misunderstanding on your part.

However, sometimes it would be corporate suicide to approach your supervisor first. In such cases, you may have to violate the organizational imperative by going directly to your supervisor's boss, to human resources, or to the company's abuse hotline. Just understand that if you do so before talking with your supervisor, you will be taking a risk.

Abuse Hotlines

Abuse hotlines are fine for companies to have. That does not mean they are necessarily taken seriously by the company or are any different from any other effort by companies to keep employee disputes *all in the family*. Like any other means companies establish to receive employee complaints, they are worth the value the company invests in them to seriously receive, consider, and rectify employee complaints. They should not, however, be considered a substitute for rational strategies to remain employed. Nor should you presume they will automatically protect you from retaliatory acts by those who are the subject of your report. Only in companies in which upper management gives active support to those hotlines can the promise of protection from retaliation carry any real weight.

Support Your Immediate Supervisor

The next most important rule for you to follow is to support your immediate supervisor. It is not enough to merely refrain from being an active antagonist of your supervisor to survive. If you do not demonstrate an attitude of active support for your boss, he or she will start viewing you with disfavor. He or she will become suspicious that either you do not think he or she is a good supervisor or that you want his or her job. You will be particularly vulnerable if you are an excellent employee.

There is a direct correlation between the degree of active support you must demonstrate and your performance. The better your performance, the more support you must demonstrate. Otherwise, jealousy will seed. If you are a peak performer, your boss wants you to make him or her look good. He or she will be threatened if he or she thinks you are performing well to advance your own interests. Only if you satisfy your boss's desire that you make him or her look good will you be able to stave off the natural jealousies that will inevitably result.

REMAIN FLEXIBLE

The third most important rule for you to follow, particularly if you have long tenure, is to remain flexible. If your long-term manager is replaced, you will not be given more than six months to demonstrate that you will be a team player for your new boss. If you take on the attitude that the new boss does not know what he or she is doing or if you appear to resist changes from the past ways of doing things, your new boss will conclude that you are not someone that can help him or her succeed. Instead, you will need to find ways to express early and often your support for the inevitably different direction your new boss will be taking. You will need to have your new boss come to believe that he or she can use you in his or her new team.

NEVER THINK YOU ARE GOOD ENOUGH

The fourth rule is you should never think your level of performance is good enough. What may have been acceptable or even very good performance in the past may be viewed as stagnated performance now. That is particularly true in the current economic climate. In some companies today, you are only as good as your current performance. Only good performers are removed from those selected for layoff purposes. Do not rely on the esteem in which you were held by the ghosts of past supervisors. Remain innovative. Always be looking for ways to improve processes, cut costs, and make your boss's overall performance look better. Never quit making yourself indispensable.

YOUR SUPERVISOR CAN SAVE YOU

The fifth and last rule for you is that if you get into trouble with your supervisor, the number one person who can save you in the organization is that very same supervisor. Remember the organizational imperative—each rung of the organization needs to be supported by the next lower one or else the organization collapses. So do not expect, even when you are right, that your supervisor's boss will support you. Nor will human resources take your side the great majority of the time. Unless you are the president's nephew, or a well-placed mentor is willing to facilitate the resolution of a dispute between the two of you (which can be viewed as going outside the chain of command), in order to remain employed by the organization, you will have to deal with the new boss.

In a small minority of the cases in which a new boss comes into an organization and creates havoc, the employer soon replaces them. If your new boss is that bad and you maintain low visibility and let others be the focus of his or her negative attention, you may have a chance to outlast his or her tenure.

More often, though, you will have to deal with the new boss yourself. You either cooperate and support the boss or get out. It is often hard to know how to go about cooperating. Some new bosses get the lowdown on new employees and make judgments about them so quickly that there is no real chance for the subordinate to turn things around for the better. In such cases, it is best to simply buckle down and try to comply with the new boss's requests—no matter how unreasonable—while quietly exploring options outside the company.

Strategies for First-Line, Nonunion Supervisors

By far the most vulnerable employee in the organization (and the most difficult to save) is the first-line, nonunion supervisor. This is because that person is situated at the lowest rung of the nonunion management totem pole, is the least powerful amongst managers, and that person takes the brunt of any organized opposition by the nonmanagement workforce. In effect, the first-line supervisor is often caught in a pincer between the hourly workforce and higher level management.

Vulnerability as a first-line supervisor is ironic, because frequently the labor unrest that causes a first-line supervisor's demise is a product of simply carrying out the instructions he or she was given. Higher level managers often value the drill sergeant first-line supervisor who is willing to crack down on what upper management considers a lazy and lax production crew. Management's assessment of that value, however, is soft and malleable, and is subject to rapid conversion to harsh disfavor if, for example, a handful of hourly workers begin to complain about the supposed abusive management style of the first-line supervisor.

Therefore, the basic watchword for you as a first-line supervisor is do not be fooled into thinking that you have the unwavering support of management, no matter what they say. As soon as you represent a liability, in whatever terms management defines, you will be considered expendable. In a union shop environment in which the specter associated with the cost and disruption caused by the filing of numerous grievances can be intimidating to management, the speed of your potential conversion from perceived asset to perceived liability accelerates. Generally, however, the weakness of your position corresponds inversely with the strength and influence of the labor force under your supervision.

Therefore, while you must support the orders you are given, you also must always attempt to retain good relationships with the hourly workers whom you supervise. Indeed, apart from the consequences of not, it will make your life easier if you do that anyway. The problem is that it only takes a small number of hourly workers, particularly popular ones, to get you in trouble. Sometimes, once trouble starts, you will be lucky to have a faction of hourly workers step forward to support you. Even if the hourly workers who are criticizing you are known incompetents and malcontents, do not count on other union witnesses to dispute their reports about your mistreatment of them. *Union workers will not rat out other union workers.*

What else should you do? If you are given direction to whip a unit into shape and weed out any marginal performers, you must at all times communicate the steps you are taking with your supervisors, and obtain and document their assent to proceed. Coordinate with human resources to ensure that you are doing it the right way—and not in a manner that human resources can later say you should have known would lead to labor unrest and untold grievances.

In the same vein, if you have a particularly sticky disciplinary problem you need to address, it is a good idea that the company—usually through human resources—involves the union business agent or shop steward. They should let the union know well in advance what steps you plan to take. Keep human resources in the loop so it can do that. In this way, you will reduce the probability that any complaints that are made by a few unsatisfied poor performers are magnified by the union into claims that your mismanagement adversely affects the entire work unit.

Strategies for Commissioned Salespersons

Some of the highest paid workers in the world are not managers, they are commissioned salespersons. Sometimes that is their undoing. It is not infrequent that they earn more than their salaried managers who accepted that position because they did not match the success of their subordinates. The jealousies that grow out of that unnatural condition have been the demise of many commissioned salespeople.

How can that happen? First, the accounts belong to the company, not the salesperson. Except in cases in which contracts provide otherwise, the employer can redistribute those accounts as it so desires. That means your boss can mess with you. The disputes that follow each territory or account redistribution, or the announcement of a change in your compensation plan, often become shouting matches over who has a right to do what. You will seldom win those disputes. Your supervisor is the boss—not you. Even the best salesperson, who takes their case to the president of the company seldom obtains satisfaction because, simply speaking, the president cannot allow the sales staff to run the company.

In assessing how far to go to push your grievance, consider whether higher management had a hand in the pending changes in commission, territory, or account restructuring. The higher up the decision chain reaches, the lower your chances of getting the company to reverse course. Usually, the best you can hope for in such cases is an *accommodation* in the form of a promised reassignment back to you of a key account, a promise to assign you the next substantial account, or a delay before putting into effect the new reduced commission structure.

Sometimes, the changes management makes to commission structures, accounts, or territories substantially reduces the compensation of a company's sales staff. If you believe management has been unfair to you as a commissioned salesperson, your best option may be to leave the company for a more remunerative position elsewhere. In the meantime, it is best to maximize your productivity and demonstrate to your current employer that while you respectfully disagree with the changes, you can roll with the punches. That way, you keep your job and take the money while you look for other employment.

If, on the other hand, management has changed the commission structure for the specific purpose of depriving you of a particularly large earned commission, or purports to change the compensation plan retroactively, you may have a legal claim. Talk to a lawyer.

Strategies for Nonunion, Hourly Workers

This group, more than any other group of workers, is less subject to the threat of employment destabilization by political deception or internal jealousies. They are less subject to layoffs than the multiple levels of mid-level managers that exist. They are not the target of hostile board members who blame them personally for the company's poor profit and loss performance. In other words, relative to other more vulnerable employees, they are the stealth employees. As a result, they have only one person to please—their supervisors.

Theoretically, it is simple for you as an hourly worker to succeed because your supervisor will be pleased if you do two things—show up on time consistently and produce. However, there are also two things that can undermine that theoretical simplicity—you and your co-workers.

Doing the job is not solely a question of putting up good numbers. You must also have a good attitude towards your supervisor, the company, the work, and your co-workers—generally in that order. Regardless of your numerical performance, if you are perceived to be a *smart alec* or tend to buck your supervisor, you will not do well in a corporate environment. That may not be all bad. Other options are available to you. Go work for yourself if you have a problem with authority. You will probably make a lot more money and be happier.

However, even if you have everything else working for you, your employment may be sabotaged by hostile cliques and antagonistic co-workers. An office or production facility is a natural place for alliances to form both for and against a particular worker. Sometimes, being the new kid on the block (especially a talented one) is cause enough for some co-workers to attempt to see to it that you do not succeed. They can do this by refusing you training, failing to cooperate with you, actively sabotaging your work, or complaining to the boss about you or your work.

Therefore, the first thing you must do if you are placed in a new work unit is get the lay of the land. Watch carefully to see who is in what group and what the pecking order is. Try to be inclusive and friendly to everyone. It is particularly important that you start up some kind of friendship with at least one person in each group, so that if someone in the group starts *bad-mouthing* you, there will be someone there to defend you or blunt the criticism.

Sometimes a new employee is tested by a clique and is given a hard time to see what he or she is made of. The biggest mistake you can make at that point is to go running to management with your problem. That only shows the group that you are thin-skinned and a rat who cannot be trusted. Instead, let any initial hazing roll off your back, except where the harassment takes the form of unlawful discrimination. In that event, you should report it immediately to human resources. Regardless of the high likelihood that report would generate retaliation, it is far easier for you to justify making the report. Any retaliation that follows would likely not be severe or long-lasting, because your report would be seen, even by many members of the adversarial clique, as justified.

Strategies for Probationary Employees

If you are a new employee hired under a probationary period, can you be terminated without cause, for any reason? Technically, the short answer is no. A probationary employee may not have the same degree of protection as those who have completed their probationary period, but it is incorrect to say a probationary employee can be terminated for any reason. Rather, like any other at-will employee, a probationary employee cannot be terminated for a reason that violates the law. That could include a termination for an unlawful discriminatory reason, such as race, sex, age, national origin, religion, or disability, or for a reason that violates public policy, such as for filing a workers' compensation claim or for objecting to illegal misconduct.

Survival Tips

For Executives

- ✦ Assess the strength of your opposition.
- ✦ Intervene if necessary to prevent the strength of your opposition from growing.
- ✦ Assess the strength of your supporters.
- ✦ Count and rank your supporters.
- ✦ Use your supporters to win support with neutral players.
- ✦ Use your supporters to flip weak opponents.

For Mid-level Managers

- ✦ Stay within your chain of command.
- ✦ Support your supervisor.
- ✦ Remain flexible.
- ✦ Never think your performance is good enough.
- ✦ Remember, your number one potential rescuer is the supervisor who threatens you.

For First-Line Supervisors

- ✦ Do not count on your employer's unwavering support.
- ✦ Always retain good relationships with the hourly workers you supervise.
- ✦ Before taking action against your subordinates, document your employer's assent that you proceed, and bring human resources into the loop.
- ✦ Inquire if the union leadership should be informed of what you intend to do.

For the Hourly Worker

- ✦ Get the lay of the land and discern whom you must impress.
- ✦ Be inclusive and friendly to your co-workers.
- ✦ Perform with accuracy and dependability.
- ✦ Perform with a positive, team-oriented attitude.

Chapter 4

Using HR to Survive Abuse at Work

Most employers of any size have a human resources department or director. Typically, this department is responsible for recruiting, testing, hiring, training, and providing line managers with guidance on employee discipline and termination matters. It is also typically designated as the department employees should go to if they feel they are being discriminated against or unfairly treated.

Your Need to Report Harassment

You can imagine that it can become somewhat confusing to a human resources officer to one day hear from a manager that he or she would like to fire you and hear from you the next day about how you think that manager is unfair and discriminatory. In such cases, you should be aware that any apparent conflict is usually resolved in favor of line management and against you. This is not because human resources staff are bad people—it is just that most human resources officers have a keen sense of survival. Except in the most extreme and obvious cases of unlawful management behavior, most would not be able to survive in the organization if they supported employees over managers.

Still, the United States Supreme Court has ruled that if you do not take your complaint of discrimination to human resources, you may lose your ability to sue your employer for on-the-job harassment under certain circumstances. Further, at the time you have something to complain about, you may not know what track record your manager has with the company or if your manager is already in jeopardy of being fired because of similar past bad behavior. You would typically not be familiar with how powerful or principled the human resources representative is in dealing with employee complaints. Some are thoroughly principled and are well-supported by the highest echelons of management, so that they have equal footing with line managers in the organization. There is always the chance that the human resources representative takes such complaints seriously. This kind of representative will investigate the matter fully and fairly, will not shy away from reaching conclusions that favor employees over management, and is not afraid to put conclusions uncomplimentary to management in writing.

Regardless of how small the chance of that happening, you will usually be well-advised to take that chance and report management's wrongdoing to human resources. For one thing, if you report it, the matter might be resolved in your favor. For another, should the matter later lead to litigation, a jury will expect that you made such a report. Think about it: if you do not report it, are later terminated, and it comes out at trial that the employer had a clearly defined complaint procedure that you ignored—and the company later fires the manager over a similar incident—you could lose your case altogether.

Instead, you need to portray yourself to a jury as a worker who is cooperative, longsuffering, and a team player who will follow management's advice and direction in reporting serious matters as they occur. To that end, it would further that portrayal to ensure management is placed on notice of the offense against you and is given a fair opportunity to correct the situation. If after fair notice management fails to act, you will have no shared responsibility for its inaction.

Using Good Judgment in Reporting Harassment

Nothing will frustrate a human resources representative more than an incessant stream of reports of trivialities. You will need to exercise good judgment in reporting misdeeds. Only do so when it is prudent. In making that judgment, consider:

+ the seriousness of the offense;
+ whether it is the first or a repeated offense;
+ whether witnesses can corroborate the occurrence;
+ whether there is any other way to verify the offense occurred;
+ the impact the offense has on your work;
+ the likelihood that if you do not report it the offense will recur;
+ whether the manager has a past history of other similar acts;
+ your knowledge of human resources' reputation as a department in the organization that deals fairly with employee complaints;
+ your knowledge of the human resources representative's reputation for integrity in dealing with such matters; and,
+ how near you are to the end of your capacity to cope with the harassment without third party intervention.

In most cases, employees tend to underreport. This is principally because of their fear of retaliation. Typically, that is a consequence of having a weak human resources department that depreciates or mishandles those complaints and too frequently allows acts of retaliation to occur. Employees know that even when confidentiality is promised, it is seldom delivered. Sometimes a complainant learns even before returning from human resources to their work station their boss has been given a heads-up by human resources that the complainant dropped in. Even when he or she is not overtly sabotaged by human resources, his or her identity as the complainant will likely come out. Even if he or she is not named as a complainant by human resources, sufficient facts about the complaint will need to be revealed to the manager so that he or she can respond. That gives the manager a pretty good idea of who made the complaint.

Even when the human resources department attempts to protect the complaining employee from retaliation by putting the manager on administrative leave during the investigation and warning the manager not to retaliate, retaliation still happens. Sometimes the manager waits to perpetrate retaliation until long after the close of the investigation, in an attempt to obscure the causal connection between the retaliation and the complaint. Sadly, as long as you continue to work for the same manager it will not be too difficult for that manager to find *legitimate* fault with you, because no one is perfect. Everyone makes mistakes. Managers who look for mistakes can find and magnify them if they are so inclined.

Retaliation can follow even if the offending manager is terminated. For example, if a male manager is terminated for sexual harassment, his pals will resent the one who caused him to be terminated. That resentment can be played out in the form of active retaliation through mean and hostile treatment, or an unwillingness to continue to assist, train, or cooperate with the complainant, thereby causing him or her to fail. Only you can gauge the seriousness of the offense and your consequent need to report it. Just because you think someone else would not think it was serious, you should not be deterred if the matter is serious to you. Otherwise, you stand the risk that unreported offenses of that kind would be repeated and would either somehow injure you or drive you out of the company.

Sometimes an offense seems trivial at its first occurrence, but it takes on an entirely different cast if it occurs repeatedly. The frequency of occurrence of those incidents is an important factor that helps human resources understand that the matter is a serious one that needs to be dealt with. Further, if the offender has a history of prior similar offenses towards others, it does not take as much convincing of the human resources staff that the matter needs to be dealt with, for the perpetrator is at it again. Indeed, if you delay reporting, it could have the negative effect of causing human resources to conclude that the offender had a *relapse* and just needs reminding. In contrast, if you report a first offense soon after a similar encounter was reported by someone else, it could persuade human resources that the offender is *continuing* the unacceptable behavior and must be terminated.

The Trick is to Change the Subject

Through your reporting efforts, the trick is to change the subject. You want to move the perception from having to deal with your complaints to the offender's refusal to listen to human resources' admonitions. Once you have been able to engage human resources and it has issued directives and admonitions to the offender, any repeat offenses will be taken as an affront to human resources' authority. Most offenders cannot help themselves. They will do it again. Once it becomes an authority issue between human resources and the offending manager, you have won.

Verifying Complaints

If there are favorable witnesses to support your report, human resources' willingness to automatically take the manager's word over yours will be somewhat moderated. Most offenders are not stupid, and will take care not to commit offenses in the presence of third parties. In other cases, a particularly bold, arrogant, or impatient offender may commit his or her offenses openly, almost as if to dare the victim or others to challenge him or her. Even when witnesses exist, however, *witnessing* is hard to come by. Perhaps a good friend will be willing to stand shoulder to shoulder with you. More often, however, those people have jobs to protect. Unless they are also being threatened, they may be reluctant to step forward with you. Still, in an environment with a strong human resources department, you would be surprised how some human resources representatives encourage, and indeed, protect, witnesses who cooperate with their investigation.

Apart from live witnesses, other means are available to a creative and aggressive human resources department to verify complaints. Some employees have notes of conversations and events. There may be physical evidence these events occurred, such as a videotape, a telephone tape recording (where legal), an email or voicemail, a personal note or card from the offender, or a job order that the offender has changed to sabotage the productivity of the employee.

On other occasions, the verification could be through information imparted by the offender to the employee. For example, if the employee claims the offender was sexually harassing him or her and that they received an invitation to the cabin on the lake because the offender's spouse is out of town, that information contains facts that can be verified. If they can be verified, that suggests the employee was telling the truth. Otherwise, why would they possess that confidential information?

Verification that the offense occurred through independent witnesses or some other means is important, because a great deal of pressure will be exerted on the human resources official to simply find that he or she cannot substantiate the complaint. That is the result that often follows, because otherwise the human resources representative's report could become *Exhibit A* in the employee's wrongful discharge suit if things go sour later. Human resources representatives learn early on not to be so foolish as to generate liability against their employer by writing reports that substantiate unlawful conduct occurred.

Considerations that Affect Your Reporting Decision

Your capacity to defer reporting, even of matters that stand the risk of seeming to be trivial, will be influenced by how greatly your work is affected by them. Sometimes it is not the act, but the effect of the act, that determines when to report. If you are being distracted into creating errors by icy stares, you may have no choice but to report something that cannot be well-described, let alone corroborated, or else your unexplained poor work product that follows will be your undoing. If you complain only after the harassment has had its effect by causing you to put out substandard work, any later complaint about that conduct will be viewed with suspicion and taken to be a defensive ploy on your part, devoid of substance.

Sometimes an offense stands little chance of being repeated, because it was entirely out of character for the perpetrator to have committed it. In such cases, you have a choice in the matter. You can report it and get the person in trouble. However, if this was that person's first and only offense, it is hardly likely the person will come away with serious discipline. If the act is never repeated, what have you gained but to reap the enmity of the person you report to and his or her friends? Sometimes you benefit from the good will you generate with the offender and your co-workers by letting acts go that you believe are clearly one-time only offenses.

On other occasions, you may have seen that you or others have already given the perpetrator his or her free bite, only to see that person encouraged by the belief that their conduct could continue with impunity. In those cases, you maximize the risk the conduct will be repeated by your failure to report.

Overriding all the other factors is your capacity to withstand the harassment further. At some point—in terms of your own financial interest—you will have nothing left to lose by making the report, because if you do not, you will have to quit anyway. In terms of your own health interest, at some point it becomes injurious to continue to subject yourself to that harassment. Again, only you can determine when you have reached that point. If you believe you have reached it, do not let the offender win by just quitting. At least report it and give the employer notice it is occurring—no matter how skeptical you are about the results.

Tips for Dealing with Human Resources

1. Human resources staff are just human and must support management where they can.
2. Promises of confidentiality by human resources may not be kept.
3. Promises that you will not experience retaliation may prove false.
4. Unless you report it, you may disqualify your case from legal protection.
5. If you report harassment, it is possible that the matter could be resolved in your favor.
6. Be judicious in what you report.
7. Report it without fail when you have nothing left to lose and would quit if the conduct continued.
8. If the reported conduct continues, report it again.
9. If you experience retaliation, report that too.
10. Your objective is to move the issue away from your complaints to the offender's refusal to comply with human resources' directives.

Chapter 5

Strategies to Preempt or Prevent an Anticipated Termination

Despite your best efforts to change your relationship with your supervisor, you believe you are about to be terminated. Perhaps you were told by your supervisor to expect to be terminated unless your performance improved, and he or she has subsequently told you it has not. Perhaps you notice a change in your boss's behavior toward you that causes you to believe you will be terminated. Or perhaps you have a well-informed friend who was told it was coming down. Regardless of the source of that information, you are concerned that you are about to be fired. So, what should you be doing?

The answer depends on your situation. Preliminarily, although you may think the ax is about to fall, it is usually a mistake to bet on supposition. You do not want to jump the gun and cause your employment to be shortened based on assumptions. On the other hand, you should not ask your boss if you are going to be fired. That would only remind him or her of the power he or she has to fire you. However, if you have solid information that the termination is coming down, you do have some options.

If you sense an impending termination, you have to decide whether to preempt it or attempt to prevent it. You can preempt it through a carefully fashioned offer to resign on stated conditions. You can attempt to prevent it through a variety of strategies. These may include performance that demonstrates submission to your supervisor's authority, involving a third party agent to intervene to facilitate a resolution, or engaging in a political war. Each case stands on its own. It is a good idea to consult with an experienced employment lawyer before deciding upon a strategy.

Strategy 1: Preempt it by Proposing that You Resign

If you can accept losing your job, but cannot stand it right now, approach your boss with a proposal that you resign, but at some future date, to try and avoid an immediate termination. This might be an attractive option for you if you need more time to land a job elsewhere, or if some stock options or a 401(k) account is about to vest.

To offer to resign on stated terms could also be a desirable strategy if you have an overwhelming need to lessen the stress you are feeling from an impending termination. Typically, once you indicate your willingness to go, that will appease your supervisor. Your supervisor may feel gratified you spared him or her the unpleasantness associated with the final stages of termination. He or she may be more predisposed to provide you with additional time on the payroll while you are looking for work. He or she may perhaps even be more willing to provide a severance payment to you at the time of the effective date of resignation.

To perfect that strategy, you would need to schedule a time to meet with your boss personally. Emails will not do for something like this. At the meeting, get right to it and ask, "Why don't I do us both a favor, and look for a job outside the company?" At that point you will typically hear a big sigh of relief from across the table. But your job is not done. Your goal is to negotiate for the maximum amount of job-search time you can. If your employer does not view you as one whose continued employment would create morale, productivity, or security problems, they may be persuaded to give you a reasonable amount of time to secure another position. Indeed, if you are popular with your co-workers, your boss may conclude it is in the company's best interest to put a good public face on the separation and leave the impression with your co-workers that both sides are happy with the outcome.

If you have not yet started a job search, before you meet with your boss and pursue this strategy, it would be prudent for you to obtain information from a professional headhunter about how long it will be for you to be able to secure other employment. You may learn that it would take longer than your boss would allow and that you would rather try to extend your employment in other ways. One way may be by forcing the company to go through its progressive discipline steps. On the other hand, if you find it could take six months, for example, your boss may be amenable to a ninety-day deferred resignation with a three-month severance package at the end of that period. Even if you cannot nail down 100% of your optimum package, you may be able to get 70-80% of it through this method. Providing your supervisor with third party information from a reliable source would give your supervisor support for granting your request for severance he or she can use with higher-ups to justify the concession.

If you proceed with this strategy, there are other things to consider. In many states, you lose your unemployment benefits if you voluntarily quit without good cause. If you have a choice to remain employed at the time of your resignation, you may not qualify for those benefits. If your employer supports the position that you would not have had the opportunity to work for the company any longer than that, then generally you will not lose your benefits.

So, at the time of your discussion with your boss, it should be agreed that for unemployment purposes, you will have resigned *in lieu of termination*, and that your employer will not contest your application for unemployment benefits. Be sure to check with an attorney in your state to ensure you will qualify for benefits in that jurisdiction under these circumstances.

In addition, you may be able to negotiate a favorable letter of recommendation and favorable job references. Employers do not hire people on the basis of letters of recommendations. However, a good one can help get your foot in the door. If you are able to have your employer agree to provide you with one, be sure it is written to your satisfaction before you sign any formal agreement ending your employment. You may be able to submit a first draft yourself for review. It should be submitted to the person who is most logical in the eyes of the outside world to provide such a letter. If that person has some concern about its content, let them author a second draft, incorporating what they will of your ideas. Hash out any remaining differences together. Attach the letter to the severance agreement. Provide in the agreement that the employer will provide the letter, and in responding to employer inquiries, will comport with the substance of its content. (For further ideas about the content of your severance agreement, see Chapter 9.)

Strategy 2: Demonstrate Submission

If you want to avoid the termination, and possibly take legal action if you cannot, what should you be doing? The first and best way to avoid a termination is to comply with your boss' performance and/or conduct demands, no matter how unreasonable. This may seem obvious. However, a fair percentage of terminations could be avoided if the employee simply demonstrated submission to their supervisor's authority. In many cases, it was that refusal to submit that escalated the situation to a level of crisis in the first place.

Once it becomes a struggle for authority, your boss will always win. Your boss has the authority and you do not. Employees are often surprised, however, how fast their boss relents once they appropriately demonstrate their willingness to submit.

Strategy 3: Enlist Third-Party Assistance

The next possible strategy to employ is to solicit the assistance of some internal third party. Most often this will be human resources, but it can be another supervisor, your boss' supervisor, or the president of the company. Sometimes, if you present your side of the story to a third party within the organization, that person can take action to serve as an investigator, or better yet, as a facilitator or ombudsman to mediate an internal dispute.

Most often, you will be speaking to human resources, because that is the group in most organizations into which the company wishes to funnel such matters. It is also the group that is most professionally equipped to deal with a complaint. A company always takes a risk when it allows an ill-trained line manager to handle a sensitive personnel matter. For example, depending on the sophistication of your boss' supervisor, that person could—from lack of training—mishandle a sexual harassment complaint by calling the complainant and harasser together and simplistically telling them they should just get together and work it out. Most human resources professionals would be appalled by that approach.

Sometimes, however, an enlightened employee-oriented manager above your supervisor, who has developed a reputation as a person who is fair to employees, is the one to speak with. Most of the time, that person will redirect you to human resources. However, under some circumstances—particularly in smaller organizations where the human resources organization is not so well-developed—that manager may feel comfortable handling the controversy. Again, a personal appeal is required. The advantage of this approach is that you do not lose the profile of an employee who is not an immediate threat to the organization.

Strategy 4: Assume a Legal Posture

Another strategy for you to employ is a legal strategy, whether by involving a lawyer or by filing an administrative complaint of discrimination with a civil rights enforcement agency. Generally, you only want to direct a lawyer to intervene when you have nothing left to lose. Before calling attention to this strategy, there are several things you need to know.

First, once you hire a lawyer to help you fight the organization, your long-term career with that company is over. A lawyer's letter may save your job in the short-term, but you will be viewed as a threat to the organization from that time forward. As soon as they are able, your employer will rid itself of you one way or another.

Second, juries do not like lawyers either. If your case leads to litigation, a jury may believe that because you hired a lawyer before your termination—particularly if you did not first go to human resources or another supervisor—what happened afterwards was all a setup. They may believe that the lawsuit is not really yours, but your lawyer's.

Third, once you hire a lawyer, if only to write a letter, people begin to say all sorts of unfounded things about you—such as, you are suing the company—even when that was not your plan at the time. To pursue this option would stimulate events to occur that would be outside your control. It is even possible that the events that unfold could adversely affect your marketability for other employment.

Decide to pursue this strategy only after consulting with a lawyer. It may be that you should not pursue it because you have no legal leverage. If, however, you find you do have legal leverage, lean heavily on your lawyer as to whether to pursue it and how.

Your lawyer may feel that your case is so apparent that a respectful but firm lawyer letter is the best way to fend off the supervisor. Most corporations appreciate being given the opportunity to avoid potential legal problems. However, if it appears human resources has already had a hand in planning your demise and would not likely respond favorably to your lawyer's letter, filing a complaint with a civil rights enforcement agency would be the best first step to take to demonstrate your heightened level of commitment to legal action.

(For how to locate a lawyer experienced in employment law, see Chapter 10. For information about filing an administrative complaint with a civil rights enforcement agency, see Chapter 17.)

Strategy 5: Engage in a Political War

As a default strategy, when you have no legal course to pursue; you cannot identify a third party who is in position to effectively intervene; and, no amount of subservient performance could save you, a final strategy is to take the supervisor on politically. However, this course is fraught with danger. Only in the most extreme cases of supervisor harassment, such as when the supervisor has a long and well-documented history of similar abusive treatment of others, can this strategy work. Further, this strategy can only be successful if you are joined in your battle by a significant number of co-workers.

To upper management, it cannot be about you and your supervisor. The issue must be your supervisor's treatment of *others*—plural. The probability of success for this strategy is related to your employer's perception of the degree of labor unrest your supervisor will cause if left employed. The more organized the nonmanagement workforce and the more likely your employer will have to expend its funds combating multiple grievances, the more vivid the imperative will appear to your employer that your supervisor must go.

To pursue this strategy risks everything. It may hasten your termination. It may sacrifice even neutral references. It may make your employer so hostile towards you that it becomes personally involved in seeing to it that you are not soon employed elsewhere in your community (if it can help it). Even so, in rare cases, even two or three workers, acting together, who report the misdeeds of a supervisor who is a known abuser, may serve as the proverbial last straw an employer needs to rid itself of the offender.

Chapter 6

Managing an Imminent Termination

Despite your best efforts, a termination is about to happen. There are things you can be doing in anticipation to manage the crisis. There are also actions to avoid.

Ensure Your Performance is Documented

You can ensure your performance is documented in two ways—by memorializing ongoing performance and by creating an available repository for that documentation. You can memorialize your performance by making sure there is a documentary trail of memos or emails that confirm you have done the work and done it on time. You can create an available repository by ensuring that, as a practice, you retain hard copies of those memos and emails.

Do not take documents you are not authorized to have. To do so could jeopardize your ability to recover full damages at trial or could cause you to lose your case altogether. However, knowing what you are authorized to have is a bit tricky. Unless you provide your own supplies and photocopier, almost everything at work that you did not bring from home is the property of your employer. More and more frequently, employers will require terminated employees to sign acknowledgments at the time of termination that they have returned all company property in their possession. Other employers are more lax and do not have employees account for every scrap of paper they have retained. In the latter case, if your employer has allowed you to make and keep personal copies of your work product over the years, as well as your employer's feedback about your work product, those retained papers can serve as documentation.

In companies where you are allowed to keep virtually nothing at the time of termination, you could do yourself and your lawyer a favor if, in anticipation of an impending termination, you made a log of key documents. These documents should include those that prove your good performance and disprove the bogus contentions you anticipate your employer will raise. In your log, identify each document by date, parties, subject, content, and location. If it has a special form number or has a special name, note it. Your lawyer would then be able to use that log to specify the documents your employer is to produce during litigation.

Begin a Narrative of Events

While your memory is still fresh, it is important that you begin a chronological narrative of events. It is particularly important that you do so as soon as you believe you will be terminated. Termination usually involves the employer's spin of recent events. If you have carefully recorded the real version of what happened leading up to your termination in the greatest of detail, it can later be used to reveal the falsity of your employer's explanation for your termination. If you have already retained an attorney, he or she will probably ask you to start such a narrative. If you write at the top of the first page "To My Attorney," it will be sufficient to make your narrative *privileged*. This puts it outside the realm of review by your employer's attorneys later on during litigation.

In your narrative, it is important to include:

+ when you started work;
+ how you performed early on;
+ when it was that your employment took a turn for the worse;
+ to what you attribute that turn;
+ the basis for why you attribute it to that cause; and,
+ the significant events to date following that turn.

If there is a delay between the date you begin your narrative and the date of your termination, be sure to update your narrative during the balance of your employment. If you find that you need to update your narrative, do not make more than a quick note at work. Make your detailed notes at home after work so people do not become suspicious that you are writing about them, and do not therefore avoid you. But be sure to make the notes on a same-day basis. Jurors are most impressed by notes that they believe were made closely following the events they purport to describe. Do not use your employer's computer equipment to create or update your narrative. Even if you delete it, the employer might be able to recover it on its hard drive.

Make a List of Witnesses

In addition to your narrative, your attorney would appreciate having a list of any witnesses you believe could help your case, with full names, current addresses, and working telephone numbers. It will be easier to construct such a list when you are still employed and have access to employee rosters, call lists, and the employees themselves. Although during litigation your attorney will be able to serve discovery requests for such information for *Joe, the maintenance man*, by the time responses are received, Joe may have moved.

Start Networking

If you sense that your termination is inevitable, it only makes sense to begin a job search. It is always easier to find work when you are already employed. That way, in filling out job applications that require you to list your employment history, you can leave the space provided for you to state the ending date of your most recent employment blank. That eliminates questions, and shows that you are a keeper. As importantly, it will help give you perspective. There is a bigger world outside your own particular corporation. But until you actually explore it, that may be hard to realize. Once you do realize it, your last few days of dealing with your oppressive work environment will become more bearable.

Consider Consulting with an Attorney

If you have not already done so, at this point you may wish to consider consulting with an attorney to review your case and coach you through what may be the final days of your employment. As partners, you can discuss the various strategies that may still be available to you to attempt to keep or extend your employment. If you have done a careful job of selecting a lawyer, it may be that because of your lawyer's special knowledge of this employer, other options become available.

For example, it is possible that they have handled several cases of this kind with this employer in the past and are familiar with the employer's propensity to commit this particular offense. Or, it may be that because of their past successful track record with this employer, your employer may be amenable to a deal you had not even thought about. Even without that special history, it would be prudent for you to connect with an employment lawyer to see if you are on the right course and that you are doing everything you should be doing to advance your own interests.

This is all new to you. You will be getting a lot of advice from family and friends. It is an easy matter to be misled by well-meaning advice. You should take that help as nothing more than expressions of support. Listen to your employment lawyer, and if he or she is able to free you of any misconceptions, then his or her fee has been earned. (To find an experienced employment lawyer, see Chapter 10.)

In the Meantime, Do Your Job

The best strategy for keeping your job and winning a lawsuit is the same—be the very best employee you can be. The most difficult time to do that is at the presumed end of your employment and after you have been demoralized by a supervisor. You may feel like there is no point. Do not let the employer off the hook by giving up and failing to do your job. If you let up and quit producing, that may be just the development the employer needs to justify your termination. Do not play into the employer's hands. Keep fighting for your pride, your family, and your own financial interests.

Mend Fences

While you are still employed, you have the power to influence the flavor of the future testimony of those around you. It is hard enough to win an employment case, given that all the obvious witnesses are either concerned about keeping their job or keeping good references. You do not want to make it any harder by conducting yourself in a way so as to motivate your co-workers to volunteer unfavorable information about you. Remain a team player to the very end. To the extent possible, neutralize your enemies.

Be Mindful of Any Upcoming Dates

Supervisors are strategic in the timing of their terminations of workers. On occasion, they also have help from higher-ups within the company. If a few corporate dollars can be saved, they are sometimes instructed to ensure that any terminations are effected before any upcoming dates that would make them more expensive to the company (such as a stock option vesting date or a bonus eligibility date). Terminations of salespeople are often curiously timed right before a large commission is about to come due. You would do well to be particularly sensitive to the behavior of your boss, as well as to the quality and reliability of your own performance during these periods of extreme vulnerability.

Watch Out for Traps

Although you may be right that you are about to be terminated, even your boss may not yet know when or how it will be done. He or she may not have figured it out yet. Frequently, a supervisor will remain committed to the termination within a particular time frame, but be undecided as to the excuse that he or she will use for it. Often, he or she will seize upon whatever opening you give— another tardiness, a technical violation of a company rule, or a minor deviation from some manufacturing standard that is typically overlooked. Take care to do all you can not to make your employer's case for it during periods of close scrutiny. Try to focus on your work rather than their scrutiny. Otherwise, that distraction could itself lead to mistakes that will be used against you. If your boss seizes upon a particularly weak excuse for your termination, that may present an opportunity for you to save your job by persuading human resources that you have been unfairly treated.

Review Your Employer's Benefit Offerings

If you have become disabled from performing your job due to a physical or emotional injury or condition, be sure that before termination, you apply for whatever benefits are available to you based on your status as an employee. Many large employers have short- and long-term disability plans for their employees. This insurance provides continuing income to disabled employees based upon a percentage of salary during the period of disability. The catch is that such benefits are for employees. If you wait until after you are terminated to apply, you may prejudice your ability to collect.

If you have any question about your eligibility for those benefits, the law provides that your employer must make available a *summary plan description* of the benefits. This description will tell you about your eligibility. If your disability was incurred on the job, you may also be entitled to claim workers' compensation benefits. Again, if you delay filing a claim, it can prejudice your application for benefits.

You may have declined life insurance or health coverage in the past. That may have been because your spouse's employer provided them. Since then, your spouse may have changed jobs or retired. Review the company's other fringe benefit offerings to see whether or not you should sign up for coverage. Investigate whether the group benefit can be converted to an individual benefit after employment ceases. Once you are terminated, you lose the opportunity to enroll.

Do Not Create a Sense of Impending Doom

Take care not to hasten your termination by communicating to those around you that you expect to be terminated. For one thing, you could be wrong, but you bring on a termination by your conduct. It could be (as is often the case) that—unbeknownst to you—you are only one of two or more candidates for layoff. If you begin to disengage, that could tip the scales against you. Moreover, if you project that you are out of favor, it will cause your co-workers to distance themselves from you. Finally, if you tell others you expect to be the next one to go, that can be misused at trial as your assessment that you merited termination compared to others.

Instead of creating a sense of impending doom, do the following.

+ Continue to fully engage in your job requirements.
+ Maintain routine communication.
+ Contribute in team meetings.
+ Maintain good eye contact with your supervisor and co-workers.
+ Be friendly and professional.
+ Do not depict yourself as one who is about to be cut out from the rest of the herd.

Do Not Argue Your Case to Your Co-Workers

If you feel you are on the way out, the temptation will be to try to enlist support from your co-workers about how the situation is unjust. Sometimes, employees in that position take it too far and begin to argue their case to anyone who will listen. It makes employees nervous to be lobbied like this. No one likes to be drawn into a fight. Still less do they relish feeling used as head-count in support of a cause.

If you begin to act as an advocate for your own case, it could drive some supporters away from you. If it gets back to the boss that you are causing trouble by attempting to create factions, that itself could serve as the excuse your boss was looking for to fire you. If a jury hears that you were badmouthing the boss to anyone who would listen, it would bias the jury against you.

Do Not Ask Your Boss for Reassurance

The last place to expect to obtain comfort is from the supervisor who you believe is about to fire you. Think about it. Even if your supervisor is not planning on firing you, he or she cannot promise it will never happen. On the other hand, if you go to your supervisor and ask him or her, "Are you going to fire me?" it only reminds them that they can and suggests that perhaps you think they should.

Do Not Give Up and Stop Performing

Giving up will have a negative impact not just on your case, but also your job references if you do not have a case. Most supervisors tend to place greater emphasis on recent performance when it comes time to put pen to paper and draft a reference letter. If you left projects unfinished, that will weigh heavily on toning down whatever favorable reference you might otherwise deserve. Co-workers, too, are particularly impressed by memories of your performance at the end of your employment. If you leave them with the feeling that you failed to support them, or put them in a difficult situation when you departed, it will make them witnesses against you at trial.

Do Not Engage in Desperate Defensive Measures

As a defensive reaction, some employees feel compelled to *beat the employer to the punch* and end up engaging in behavior that makes them look foolish. Some resort to filing stress claims unnecessarily, thinking they can hide from work under the cloak of a doctor's excuse. Others initiate complaints with human resources that do nothing but make them look desperate and petty.

In most cases, this self-destructive self-help could be avoided with the guidance of a good employment lawyer. If you begin to feel compelled to take some action like this, pick up the phone and call a lawyer.

Do Not Go on Vacation

More terminations are planned while employees are on vacation than at any other time. For some reason, supervisors and human resources people think vacation gives them license to hold all the secret meetings about you they want. That also gives them an opportunity to dig around in your desk, get into your computer files to learn about the status of your work, and find just the right excuse for your termination. If you can defer your vacation, it would be prudent to do so.

Do Not Just Quit

If you believe you are about to be terminated, it will be very difficult to continue working under the stress. The temptation will be to avoid further trauma by taking matters into your own hands. Before you succumb to that pressure, consult with a lawyer. There may be nothing wrong with that tack. On the other hand, it may be unwise for you to do so, as:

- ✦ you could be misreading signals;
- ✦ you could be fouling up a good case;
- ✦ you could be needlessly sacrificing continuing income; or,
- ✦ you could be placing your unemployment benefits in jeopardy.

Do Not Make Illegal Tape Recordings

It would be illegal for you to secretly tape-record in-person conversations with your boss. Moreover, most courts would exclude evidence illegally obtained. To engage in conduct of this sort would only place you and your lawyer on the defensive in a court case. It could also subject you to criminal prosecution.

In some states, a party can legally tape telephone conversations in which they are one of the participants. However, even if your state permits it, do not engage in any taping activity without first consulting a lawyer.

Do Not Access Information without Authority

If you believe you are about to be terminated, your desire to know what plans are in the works may compel you to engage in foolish behavior to attempt to find out. If you go through the papers on your boss's desk, desk drawers, or gain unauthorized entry to his or her computer files, that itself will be grounds for termination and will spoil your case.

Do Not Give Your Employer an Excuse

If you feel you are about to be terminated, you are probably right. Know that your boss will be looking for any excuse to fire you. Although you are an employee at will, your boss will be needing to give his or her supervisor or human resources some plausible reason why you are being fired. Do not commit any act that could be construed to violate your employer's code of conduct.

In this period, it will be difficult to pay appropriate respect and refrain from doing or saying something that could be construed as insubordinate. If you feel the temptation to blurt out an inappropriate comment, try not to put yourself in close proximity to your supervisor. Keep your distance and stay quiet.

Do's and Don'ts in Anticipation of a Termination

Do:

1. Ensure your performance is documented.
2. Begin a narrative of events.
3. Make a list of witnesses.
4. Start networking.
5. Consider consulting with an attorney.
6. Do your job.
7. Mend fences.
8. Be mindful of any upcoming dates.
9. Watch out for *traps*.
10. Review your employer's benefit offerings.

Don't:

1. Create a sense of impending doom.
2. Argue your case to your co-workers.
3. Ask your boss for reassurance.
4. Give up and stop performing.
5. Engage in desperate defensive measures.
6. Go on vacation.
7. Just quit.
8. Make illegal tape recordings.
9. Access information without authority.
10. Give your employer an excuse.

Chapter 7

Handling the Termination Itself

You have just been summoned to a meeting with your boss and a representative from human resources. You know the day of your termination has arrived. What should you do?

The Termination Meeting

If you are summoned to a termination meeting, you will have to attend it or you will be terminated for insubordination for your refusal to attend. If you are terminated for that insubordinate act, it would likely destroy any wrongful discharge case you had. It would break the causal connection between your protected activity or protected class status and your termination.

Unless you are a public employee with due process property rights, you will have no right to legal counsel in the meeting, except by leave of your employer. Unless you are a union worker, you will have no right to have any witness or representative present either.

It is imperative that you attend, even if alone, and be there to hear what is about to occur. In most cases, the employer will have a line manager, usually the one who is responsible for the termination decision, and at least one other person present, usually a human resources representative. Usually, too, the line manager will tell you why you have been summoned, will terminate you, and will state the reason or reasons why.

In all states except Indiana, Maine, Minnesota, and Missouri, your employer is not required to state a reason for termination. If your manager does not state a reason or is vague about it, such as—"It was time for a change" or "It was just not working out," press for a reason. If a reason is stated that you can later prove to be false, that will serve as supportive evidence in a court case. Under decided case law, to show the reason stated by the employer for termination is false raises an inference that the real reason was an unlawful one. If a reason is stated that is inconsistent with any later explanation your employer gives, that can strengthen your case as well. In some cases, if you wait long enough, the firing manager will state multiple inconsistent reasons for termination in the meeting.

Your conduct in the meeting is important. If you lose control in the meeting and curse at the firing manager or tell the manager off, that can be off-putting to a juror. He or she may feel that by taking that liberty, you have been compensated enough. Remember that anything you say would be repeated and perhaps distorted in a courtroom later on if you sue. Do not say or do anything that a defense lawyer could use at trial to rob you of the natural sympathy a jury will have for you as a terminated employee.

If you ask the reason for your termination and one is given that is patently false, it does you no harm to point that out in a respectful, informative way. For example, if the employer says you did not meet your numbers and you know you had, you can simply say, "I have a copy of my report that shows I met them. May I give that to you?" That way, the jury will see that you gave the employer every chance to correct its error. If the employer refuses your offer, a jury would be irritated at its stubbornness and wonder why it was so committed to your termination regardless of the facts.

If you are able, you can interject other topics, such as to request one last chance to perform, even if on probation. If it is prudent, state your willingness to submit to a deferred resignation while you look for work elsewhere. To avoid having a termination on your record, request time to decide whether you should submit your resignation in lieu of termination. At the point of termination, most employers will not reconsider and give you another chance. However, it does not hurt to make the request, particularly if you believe the termination was not well founded. Take care that your requests do not and could not reasonably be construed to include an admission that you had been doing anything wrong when that is not true.

At that point, most employers will want you gone right then, not at some future date. Depending on the circumstances, an employer might be willing to work with you and allow you a few weeks or months to continue working while you are actively looking elsewhere.

Many employers will give you the option of resigning in lieu of termination. If you ask for a brief period, such as twenty-four hours, to decide if that is in your best interest, many employers will allow you that time.

Often, employers will offer a terminated worker some kind of severance, if only but two weeks' pay, as an inducement to have the worker sign a release of liability to prevent future suits. It is often in the termination meeting that the severance offer is presented. Some employers split the termination meeting in two parts, with the termination message delivered by the firing manager in part one and the offer of severance delivered by the human resources representative in part two. This is done so it does not look like the severance is being offered by the firing manager as *hush money*.

Do not think that there is anything suspicious about the offer of a nominal severance under those circumstances. The offer is not an admission by your employer that it did anything wrong or that it thinks you have a case. On the other hand, if you sign a release of liability in favor of your employer, that will waive your right to sue—no matter how little you get in return. So be sure to seek legal advice before you sign.

Posttermination Winding Up

After the termination meeting, you will be told that at some point you will be allowed to pack up your personal belongings and take them away. Most often this immediately follows the termination meeting. Your employer does not want you around for long. It also does not want to stand the security risk that accompanies the termination of disgruntled workers who have access to sensitive programs and systems. Do not be offended if you are accompanied by a manager or other employee as a *witness* that you are only removing what belongs to you and to be sure you have not made an unauthorized posttermination access into the company's computer system. Your escort will probably follow you out of the building to your car to ensure that you will not make any unscheduled detours elsewhere on company property to vent your frustration in other ways. None of that constitutes unlawful conduct on the part of your employer. It has every right to protect its security interest and to control the presence of others on its property.

On the other hand, some employers become carried away in the ceremony. They can create liability through the use of overzealous security officers or by creating the false impression the terminated employee had done something seriously wrong. Each state has decided for itself what circumstances give rise to liability in such cases. Check with an experienced employment lawyer to see how far yours has gone in that area.

The Exit Interview

Some companies conduct an exit interview with its terminated workers. This is typically accomplished by having you answer questions on a one- or two-page form, in which you are asked about how you think you were treated. Sometimes, you are asked to fill out the form yourself. On other occasions, you are actually interviewed by a human resources representative, who fills out the form for you. The exit interview gives a responsible employer information it can use to detect any patterns that should cause it concern that a rogue manager is creating potential liability.

On the other hand, if you believe you have been wrongfully terminated, the exit interview can be used as a *discovery* device by the employer that can work to your disadvantage. If you feel you have been wrongfully terminated but do not say so in the exit interview, that can prejudice your case later on. On the other hand, if you express your conviction that you were illegally fired, further questions may be asked as to why you feel that way. If you give answers that in any way conflict with a later version of your story, that inconsistency may be used against you at trial.

After you are terminated, you no longer owe any duty of cooperation to your former employer. Therefore, you should try to avoid participating in an exit interview. If your employer threatens to withhold your final check unless you do, call a lawyer—that is illegal.

Your Final Check and Benefits

If you are terminated, one thing to keep in mind is to make sure you receive all the pay you have earned. Almost all states have laws that regulate the time by which you are to be paid if you are terminated. (For a listing of those laws, see Appendix B.) By the time provided under your state's law, you should be paid all of your earned income, whether in the form of salary, wages, or commissions.

Commission payments are especially tricky. Your entitlement to commissions is generally a question of what your agreement is with your employer as to how commissions are to be treated upon termination. That agreement, whether formal or informal, may dictate that you are entitled to payment for sales invoiced within the pay period. It may specify that you will not be entitled to payment until the product is shipped or until some other *magic* date. Sometimes the agreement between the parties will be based on past practice. Whatever the rules of your agreement, it is best to become familiar with those rules before you receive your final check. You do not want to have to rely on your employer at the time of termination to tell you what those rules provide. If you have the opportunity before your final check is cut, it would be a good idea to sit down with your boss to go over and agree upon the sales for which you will receive a commission payment.

Your final check should include all pay, including any overtime, that you are due. In addition, if you are entitled to reimbursement for expenses you have incurred doing business for your employer, that is the time for reimbursement as well. Further, most employers will give you a separate check for any accrued and unused vacation or personal (or paid) time off (PTO). Whether you are owed accrued and unused vacation, though, is a matter of contract between you and your employer. That contractual understanding can be express or implied, and can be based on your employer's past practice with other employees.

You may also be entitled to a *pro rata share* of any performance bonus, based on your performance to the date of termination. Many times, however, bonus programs specify that you must be employed as of the end of the fiscal year or as of the end of the bonus program to be eligible to receive any bonus.

If you are entitled to stock options, be sure that you have been granted all of the options that you have been promised. With respect to options that are already vested and can be exercised, make sure you understand by what date they must be exercised posttermination and mechanically how that can be accomplished. If you have a 401(k) or retirement plan, make sure that whatever employer contributions that are required for it to pay on your behalf have been made and are up to date. Only Indiana requires that employers notify employees of their failure to make payments to an employee benefit plan. If you wish to rollover your retirement account, inquire as to how and when that may be accomplished.

If you have an employment agreement, read it to make sure there are not any other payments or items to which you are entitled. Employment agreements and some employee handbooks often provide that at the time of termination (except for cause), you will be entitled to receive advance notice of termination. If you do not, you will receive a payment in lieu of an amount equal to your salary rate for the notice period—typically two weeks. There may also be a provision in your agreement or handbook for a severance payment. This is usually either for a specified amount or based upon a formula that is tied to your tenure, such as one week per year of service to a stated maximum number of weeks' pay.

Your agreement may also provide that in the event of termination, you will be able to retain certain items of personal property, such as the laptop computer that was purchased for you. There may also be a provision that allows you to purchase the company car you have been driving at depreciated book value or at some other fixed value. Read your agreement and handbook thoroughly to ensure you receive all you should.

You should also read the *summary plan description* of any insurance plan provided by your employer to find out if you can continue those benefits in some way. Federal legislation known as *COBRA* allows you to continue your health coverage for up to eighteen months at your expense. (You must have been employed by an employer having twenty or more employees, including independent contractors, for COBRA to apply.) In order to convert from your employer's group health plan to an individualized COBRA health plan, you will need to provide timely notice of your desire to convert within sixty days of your receipt of notice of your right to do so. In some cases, you may also have an opportunity to convert a group life insurance policy or some other benefit to an individual plan.

Posttermination Filings to Protect Your Rights

Once you are terminated, time limits will apply that specify the time within which you must assert your legal rights to pursue benefits or legal claims. If you are a union member, you may have grounds to file a grievance contesting your termination. Time limits to file a grievance as short as three days are contained in union contracts. Some discrimination statutes have a very short limitation period, such as thirty days. If you are a government worker, you may have to file a *tort claims notice* within a short period of time to preserve your right to sue. If you are an injured worker, time limits will bar your claim for workers' compensation benefits unless you file a timely claim. It would be best to see a lawyer—and if you are a union worker, to talk to your shop steward or business agent— as soon as you are terminated to learn all the time limits that apply in your case.

The Effect of Termination on Your Receipt of Benefits

Generally, unless you were terminated for cause, your termination will not adversely affect your receipt of benefits. You will be entitled to unemployment compensation even though you were terminated, unless you were terminated for misconduct. Mere nonperformance will not be deemed misconduct in most cases, unless it was in the context of an habitual error committed after repeated warnings. For a listing of the state statutes regarding disqualification for misconduct and its effect on benefits, see Appendix C. For more information about unemployment benefits, see Chapter 20.

Workers' compensation and disability insurance benefits to which you are entitled are available to you regardless of the circumstances of your termination. However, contractual benefits made available by your employer through an employment agreement, such as a contractual severance benefit, or pursuant to a *Supplemental Employment Retirement Program* (SERP) may condition receipt on a termination without cause.

Termination Tips

One of the most difficult events with which you may have to contend is to be a participant in your own termination. You will be challenged not to let your emotions get the best of you. It is important that you be cooperative and as composed as possible. It would be best to stay somewhat clinical and detached so that you remain able to accurately perceive the words that are spoken and the things that are done in the termination meeting. That would also allow you the presence of mind to take advantage of any openings your employer will allow to negotiate the terms of your departure or to get one last chance to perform. While it may be a completely devastating blow, a jury will be impressed to hear you dealt with it with dignity and style, and attempted to rise above the acts that were committed against you.

Termination Tips

If you are being terminated:

1. Do not refuse to attend the termination meeting.

2. Listen attentively at what is being said.

3. Be calm and respectful.

4. If your supervisor does not give you a reason for termination, ask for one.

5. If the reason stated is patently false and you can prove it, offer that proof.

6. Feel free to negotiate time to consider what is being proposed.

7. Avoid any exit interview.

8. Ensure that you receive all you have coming to you in your final check.

9. Read your employment agreement or employment handbook to see what other rights and benefits you have.

10. Make timely filings to protect your rights.

Chapter 8

Immediately after Your Termination

No two terminations are alike. Yet, there are some general principles to follow that will help ease the pain and confusion of the moment, reduce the chances you will do something to harm your own case, and perhaps even advance your legal interests.

Remain Calm

Do not panic. You cannot think if you panic. You will need your wits about you. One of the most critical facts that must be remembered and accurately communicated to a jury is what was said at the termination meeting. You will need to be able to listen and remember the exact words that were being used, to the extent you are able, and to accurately record as soon after the meeting as possible what was said in the meeting. If you need to excuse yourself during the meeting to regain composure, do it. If you need to call a friend or family member for support immediately afterwards, make the call.

Ask Probing Questions

In some termination meetings, the boss will stubbornly refuse to state a reason for termination. Even in the great majority of states where a reason for termination is not legally mandated, if the boss refuses to give you an answer, he or she will look callous and uncaring to jurors later on for that refusal. On the other hand, in some termination meetings, the boss engages and provides a reason. Take full advantage of any openings. If the reason stated does not make sense, say so, explain why, and ask for a response. If the response does not hold water, you will be able to testify to that effect later on. If your boss is unable to respond, you will be able to testify to that later on, too. Ask what will be happening to your position and who will be performing it. If it is being dispersed, ask why you were not retained instead of a co-worker to perform that part of it. Probe as far as your boss will let you.

Remove All Personal Belongings at Your Earliest Opportunity

Your employer may request that you box up and remove your personal belongings right then. They may prefer that you do so outside of regular work hours, so it does not create so much of a scene. Take advantage of the first opportunity to do this, before your employer goes through your desk and files, and claims your personal belongings as its own.

Relinquish All Keys and ID Badges when Requested

Whether or not you have been able to remove all of your personal belongings, you must cooperate with your employer in relinquishing all keys and ID badges that allow you access to the property. You do not want to take any chance you will be accused of trespassing or stealing property later on.

Record What was Said in the Termination Meeting

Jurors are impressed by contemporaneous notes. The termination meeting is one of the most critical events in any employment case. As soon as you are able, write down what was said in the meeting. If you are entertaining litigation, you should address the narrative "To my attorney" to attempt to maintain it as a privileged, confidential communication.

Request a Copy of Your Personnel File

Your employer probably maintains a file on each employee, and places performance reviews, disciplinary documents, and other documents memorializing the dates of your hire, probation, and termination. In many states, you can request a copy of that file. This file will be of assistance to your attorney. It may be critical in his or her decision whether to take your case or to send it to an administrative agency for investigation. In some states, you can only inspect your file. In others, you can inspect it and make notes about its contents. Obtain whatever information you can for your lawyer.

Let Your Family and Friends Take Care of You

A termination is traumatic and emotionally devastating. While you may be used to taking care of your family and being strong for them, this is the time you need to let them be there for you. They may rely on you and have problems of their own they are dealing with, but they will eagerly lend you their support. Friends, too, will appreciate your reliance. To share an experience like that will only cause your friendship to deepen.

If You Need It, Seek Emotional Counseling

If you are in need of emotional counseling, seek professional help. Your health comes first. Do not be ashamed to admit that you need professional help if you are having trouble coping with the trauma of a termination. On the other hand, in most states, in most types of cases, you do not have to seek such help to prove a case. In most cases, a jury can listen to you and assess your damages based on your testimony or the testimony of a family member. Ask your attorney whether you are in a state that requires expert testimony to establish a recoverable loss for the type of claim you will be asserting. Sometimes, it is necessary for terminated employees to seek such help before they are able to calmly tell their story to a lawyer or interview for other jobs, because of the emotional impact of the termination. If you need it, use it.

Seek Legal Advice
Only from a Knowledgeable Lawyer

Employment law is a speciality area of law. Although you may have a family friend who is a lawyer, only a lawyer experienced in employment law will be able to tell you if you have a case. (See Chapter 10 on how to find such a lawyer.)

As Soon as You are Able, Look for Other Work

A plaintiff in an employee rights case always has the obligation to show that reasonable efforts were made to mitigate (or lessen) damages by seeking other employment. Consult with your attorney about exactly what will be expected of you in terms of the geographical area of your search, the type of work you should be pursuing, and the pay range you are expected to consider acceptable.

In looking for other work, remember the cardinal rule—work is your best asset and a lawsuit is your least asset. Every lawsuit, even one that looks air tight, is risky. To the extent that you have been able to recover from the damage caused by your employer, so much the better. No responsible attorney would ever advise you to malinger or do anything but exercise your best efforts to get back on your feet. You want to become satisfactorily reemployed as soon as you possibly can.

Forget about the effect that reemployment would have on reducing your damages in a lawsuit. An attorney would much rather go into court with a client who did everything possible to become reemployed and found suitable employment within a reasonable period of time than one who remained unemployed for an inordinately long period of time under suspicious circumstances. An inexplicable period of unemployment may call into question the reliability of the plaintiff's testimony about the vigor with which reemployment was pursued. It may even taint the plaintiff's credibility generally.

Do Not Start Cutting Your Own Deal

The temptation is great, particularly for executives, to begin to negotiate their own deal in the termination meeting. The problem is that they frequently engage in self-defeating negotiating tactics, such as *Just pay the severance that is guaranteed in my contract and I'll go away*, when that was the event the employer was wanting to avoid by their termination *for cause* in the first place. But, having already disclosed their bottom line, the executive boxes in his or her lawyer, who would have wanted to start with a higher number. It is better to simply gather information and get the employer to allow you to defer a response to their offer in the termination meeting.

Do Not Release Your Employer Without Consulting a Lawyer

If you sign a *release of liability*, it means you cannot sue the released party. Except in the most extreme and outrageous circumstances, a signed release will be upheld. While most releases that are presented to employees internally caution them to seek legal advice before signing, scattered cases are still found in which a supervisor will threaten an employee that if he or she does not sign the release immediately, his or her final check will be withheld. This is illegal.

Do Not Write a Letter of Protest to the Company

Many people naively feel that if only higher-ups in the company knew the truth about what had happened, they would intervene. So they write a letter to the president of the company explaining the situation. While it is good to give the employer a chance to do the right thing, that is not usually the proper way to do so. Typically, employees who write such letters have done themselves no favor. Rambling in style, angry in tone, and vague or imprecise in asserting the real reason for termination, such letters often serve as supportive evidence for the employer at trial.

Do Not Start Writing Letters to Your Congressional Delegation

While it may seem a natural thing to do, depending on your relationship with your senator or congressperson, before you write a letter to an elected official decrying your termination, run that idea past a lawyer. Show him or her your draft. In most cases, such a letter will only do you harm. They often contain what lawyers call *admissions*, which can be used against you at trial. Worse still, sometimes they allow the employer to depict the terminated employee as a nutcase.

Do Not Engage in Physical Harm

Even if it may not completely wreck your case, if jurors heard that upon being terminated you launched into an obscene tirade, it would surely cause them to view you with far less sympathy. If you went further and breached the peace by putting your hands on your boss or running down the corridor destroying property, it would, in the eyes of most lawyers, disqualify your case from their consideration.

Do Not Remove Anything that Does Not Belong to You

If you remove anything that does not belong to you, your lawyer will be precluded from using it as evidence. In fact, your lawyer would risk disqualification if they read a confidential document that you stole from the employer. Further, if during a case it is discovered you took documents inappropriately, under the *after acquired evidence doctrine*, your employer may be able to cut off your economic damages as of the date the inappropriate action was discovered.

Do Not Refuse to Return Property Belonging to the Employer

Perhaps during employment you were issued a company car, a laptop computer, or some expensive samples. Perhaps you were allowed to work at home on a critical project and you still have the documents the company needs to complete it. Do not try to use these items as leverage to gain concessions from your employer. Whether or not your employer has wrongfully terminated you, you have an independent obligation to return the property. Return any property promptly so your employer's lawyers will not be able to put you and your lawyer on the defensive by filing counterclaims against you. Plus, you do not want the jury to be biased against you for your own bad conduct.

Do Not Immediately File an Internal, Nonunion Grievance

Many employers offer employees the opportunity to file internal grievances. Employees seldom prevail in those settings. There is a greater chance you could prejudice your case by accepting that invitation. It is only natural that each time you tell your story it will be slightly different. However, your employer's lawyer will try to paint those slight differences as glaring inconsistencies. To participate in those internal grievances only allows your employer to have you repeat your story over and over. This gives your employer's defense lawyers the opportunity to try to create inconsistencies between your various *tellings*.

Indeed, there is no assurance your statements will even be accurately taken down by the employer's representative in the internal grievance. That representative is in position to be called as a witness for the employer at trial to rebut your testimony. By participating, your position is already somewhat compromised, because you have to admit you met with its representative and told your tale. That puts your employer in position to say you said something you did not say.

Do Not Sign a Confession

If your employer's security department has pulled you in for an interview because it suspects you of wrongdoing, it may use gestapo-type tactics to coerce a confession from you. One such tactic is to threaten criminal prosecution unless you come clean. They may put a form in front of you and tell you that all they want is something for their file and that if you sign it, they will forget the matter and not press charges. The form they make reference to may not be as innocuous as they represent. Typically, it is a confession of intentional wrongdoing, most often theft. Regardless of how sympathetic your plight, if you sign it, you will have a hard time convincing a lawyer to take your case.

Do Not Try to Handle it Alone

Your pride may be deeply wounded. You may feel ashamed that you have been terminated. You may become depressed that you have experienced what you believe to be a career ending termination. Take advantage of whatever support system is available to you. You will heal more quickly if you decide not to hibernate.

Termination Tips

Do:

1. Remain calm.
2. Ask probing questions.
3. Remove all personal belongings at your earliest opportunity.
4. Relinquish all keys and ID badges when requested.
5. Record what was said in the termination meeting.
6. Request a copy of your personnel file.
7. Allow your family and friends take care of you.
8. Seek emotional counseling if you need it.
9. Seek legal advice only from a knowledgeable lawyer.
10. Look for other work as soon as you are able.

Don't:

1. Start cutting your own deal.
2. Release your employer without consulting a lawyer.
3. Write a letter of protest to the company.
4. Start writing letters to your congressional delegation.
5. Engage in physical harm.
6. Remove anything that does not belong to you.
7. Refuse to return property belonging to the employer.
8. File an internal, nonunion grievance.
9. Sign a confession.
10. Try to handle it alone.

Chapter 9

Negotiating a Severance Agreement

It is not uncommon today for terminated employees to be offered some amount of severance upon termination, whether or not the employer has a legal obligation to pay it. Usually, the offer is conditioned upon the execution of a release agreement waiving all rights to sue. Usually, too, the offer is inadequate. So, how do you go about getting the employer to enhance the offer?

In most cases, terminated employees do not have a legal case to pursue. That is because most are employees at will, who can be terminated for any reason that does not violate a statute, public policy, or an employment contract with their employer. When there is no legal case to pursue, the terminated employee (rather than a lawyer) may be in a better position to negotiate a severance agreement. This is because there would be nothing a lawyer could say in a demand letter to give the employer or its attorney pause for concern.

How to Get More Severance

To put yourself in a better position to obtain a severance package, take the following steps. Call a prominent employment recruiter in your area, tell them who you are, what you do, how much you make, and ask them how long it will take for you to become re-employed in a position at or near what you were making. They will tell you it will likely take *x months*. Take that information back to your employer. In an in-person meeting with the decision-maker, tell him or her that you have checked around and were told by this highly respected firm that it will take you *x months* to get other work. Then say, "I cannot afford to be without income that long. I need to bridge this period with continuing pay until my next job. Is the company willing to do that?"

In that way, you are not telling the employer it has done anything legally wrong. Nor are you threatening a lawsuit. What you are doing is appealing to the employer as a matter of *equity* to assist you to ease the pain of the termination. In doing that, though, even though you did not threaten the decision-maker with lawyers or lawsuits, he or she cannot help but think that if your plea is not satisfied, you may have no choice but to run to a lawyer. In most cases, that fear gives you more leverage than anything a lawyer could say.

Even if you do have a legal case, but would be willing to forgo litigation if a sufficiently large severance is offered, it is not a bad idea to first approach the employer yourself using this tactic. Chances are, something will be offered as a result. If that amount is still insufficient, at least you can use that first offer as a base to build upon through the efforts of your attorney. That may make it easier to achieve a successful settlement because it would narrow the gap between the parties. It may also reduce your attorney's contingent fee, which may be based on the percentage the lawyer is able to negotiate on your behalf over and above what you were already offered. The key is not to ask too little in your first approach. Otherwise, you leave your lawyer no room to negotiate. It is best to coordinate any planned approach with your lawyer.

If your employer is unwilling to bridge the entire expected period of unemployment (as is typically the case) counter-propose some alternatives. Go back with a request for continuing pay for the entire period, but with a provision that if you find work, it will terminate the severance payment, or your new pay will serve as an offset. You can refine that provision further by agreeing that payments would stop only if your next job pays over a certain amount.

The Contents of Your Severance Agreement

Your severance agreement should specify the periodic amount of your continuing pay, the period over which the payments will be made, and when the payments will end. Usually, the amount will be paid out over a period of weeks or months. However, if you are able to negotiate payment of the severance up-front in a lump sum, you may be able to draw unemployment immediately. If payment is made over time, you may not be eligible to receive unemployment benefits until after the last payment is received.

In some cases, you may be able to negotiate a continuation of some fringe benefits. If fringe benefits are to be continued, it should be clear which specific benefits that includes. Typically, it would include health insurance. However, the employer may not agree to include all fringe benefits available to active employees. If you are to pay or contribute to the payment of the continuing fringe benefits, the amount of that payment or contribution should be specified.

In addition to the basic severance amount, such agreements should specify any other amounts you are to receive, including:
+ the amount of your final check;
+ your entitlement to, and the amount of, your accrued and unused vacation or personal (or paid) time off (PTO), if that is to be paid;
+ your entitlement to any future commissions;

◆ your entitlement to bonuses; and,

◆ the amount of any expense reimbursements that are due.

The agreement may also contain other economic provisions, such as whether your employer will pay for outplacement services. However, in that case, for it to simply specify that *outplacement services will be provided* does not suffice. Outplacement services can include anything from a $200 package for a review of your résumé to a $15,000 executive outplacement package. The best way to handle outplacement, if you think you need it, is to ask your employer what company it uses for outplacement services. Then, call the provider and ask what levels of service it provides and the cost associated with each level. That way, you can negotiate with your employer for the level that suits you. The agreement should then provide something to the effect that: *Employer shall provide Employee outplacement services through [specified] Agency in a sum not to exceed $__*. If your employer routinely provides outplacement, but you do not need it, try to negotiate a cash payment in place of it.

Other economic terms can include a transfer of property. Items such as a laptop computer or company car can sometimes be purchased by departing employees.

NONECONOMIC FACTORS

Noneconomic factors can be just as important as economic factors in the structure of a severance agreement. It may be important to attempt to contain the damage that has been done to you by the termination. You may be able to get your employer to agree to a *nondisparagement clause*, whereby you and your employer agree not to make any derogatory statements about the other to any third party. You may also be able to negotiate that you be allowed to resign *in lieu* of termination to protect your employment record. In that case, you would submit a letter of resignation effective the last date of your active employment. There would also be agreement that your employer would code the cessation of your employment as a resignation rather than a termination in its personnel records. Add to the agreement that the records would reflect you are eligible for rehire. The severance agreement could also contain a contractual commitment on your part that you would not apply for reemployment.

In addition to keeping your employer from saying bad things about you, it may also be important to you to require your employer to say good things about you in an agreed upon letter of recommendation. The letter should be negotiated before you sign the severance agreement and attached to it. The agreement should provide that *Employer shall provide Employee with a favorable letter of recommendation in the form submitted and signed by [Employee]*. That way, there would be no disagreement later on as to what the letter must include. You may also want to have the agreement provide that in responding to your prospective employer inquiries, your employer will not depart from the substance of the letter and will provide no other information to third parties about you.

Many companies will do nothing more than agree to comply with their policy of providing *neutral* references. That is, they will only confirm dates of employment, last position, and pay. Their thinking is that if they restrict the information they provide to objective data, they will avoid liability for defamation of character. In that case, it would be helpful if you could get your employer to promise in the agreement that it will follow its own procedure of only giving neutral references. That way, if it violates its own policy, you could sue it for breach of contract.

Other noneconomic terms may include an agreement that your employer will not contest your application for unemployment benefits. This provision is recommended, particularly when you believe your employer may later change its story to attempt to deprive you of the benefits. They may tell the authorities that you were terminated for misconduct or voluntarily left without good cause, when neither is the case.

Less typically, if you are a person in a sensitive regulatory position—such as a chief financial officer or regulatory compliance officer—and your performance is subject to an audit by a regulatory agency after your termination, you may want your employer to add a provision to protect and defend you from liability. This situation would come into play if you are named as a party in litigation brought by a government body or dissident shareholder later on. This is known as an *indemnity and hold harmless agreement*. Basically, it would provide that in the event a suit was brought naming you as a party, the company would provide a legal defense, and if necessary, pay the amount of any adverse result on your behalf.

SPECIAL CLAUSES

Your employer may have included other special clauses that you should especially watch out for. It is usually not bothersome for your employer to indicate in the severance agreement that you must comply with the confidentiality agreement that you signed when you were first hired. This may obligate you not to divulge confidential information, like pricing policies, customer lists, or trade secrets to third parties. On the other hand, some employers want to have you also agree not to compete with it for a period of time after termination. Most states regulate the validity of those noncompete clauses. They will usually be held valid if they are reasonable in terms of their limitations of time and geographic area, and meet any other technical requirements of that state's laws. Be sure to call any such clause to the attention of a lawyer. Ask whether it would be enforceable in your state, and under what circumstances.

Sometimes the definition of competing employer in those clauses is unnecessarily broad. It may be that you or your lawyer can negotiate a modification of the definition of what constitutes a *competing employer* to allow you to work without running afoul of the clause. Modifications can also be negotiated to shorten the noncompete period, restrict its geographic area, or make exceptions for a particular position with a particular employer. You may be able to eliminate it altogether.

Corporations are often initially monolithic in their approach to requiring noncompete agreements. While an employer may have a legitimate concern that a key salesperson not move clients to a competing employer, it may not have a real interest in seeing to it that someone in a staff support position goes to work for a competing employer. Yet, a noncompete clause will commonly appear in agreements for both. Taking time to point out that in your case, your employer may not really need that protection, often pays off.

If your position was one of great responsibility, you might be called upon by your former employer to testify on its behalf in future litigation. Your employer may attempt to put a provision in your severance agreement that you will cooperate with it in making yourself available to testify in future litigation. Usually, those clauses do not present a great problem. On the other hand, your lawyer will review the clause carefully to see to it that your duty to cooperate is conditioned on your reasonable availability. He or she will also take into account your responsibilities to your then current employer or your own business interests if you are self-employed. Your lawyer will take care to see that there are no unreasonable penalties for your inability or refusal to cooperate. Your lawyer will also attempt to arrange for you to be paid a reasonable fee for your time if you have to miss work or some business opportunities to provide that litigation assistance.

THE PAYOUT

Whether to receive your severance in a lump sum or over time may in part be determined by tax considerations. If you are terminated late in the year and have no immediate employment lined up, you may wish to take the severance over time so as to defer receipt of the bulk of the benefit until the next tax year. You may have to pay more of your severance in taxes if you receive a large lump sum at the end of the year. You should consult with a tax advisor or accountant to help you with that decision.

RELEASES AND VERBAL PROMISES

In all likelihood, when you are presented with your severance agreement, it will contain a clause releasing any legal claims you might have. Release agreements are valid and binding, except in the most extreme and outrageous cases of fraudulent conduct or undue duress. Do not think you can get out of the agreement easily if you sign it. Your need for the offered severance is not undue duress. Nor does the offer of such an agreement mean the employer believes it did anything wrong. It is merely a well-established conventional approach for closing out potential liability by employers.

However, because you will be presented with such an agreement, it will give you the opportunity to see a lawyer about your rights and how best to protect them. Most experienced employment lawyers will charge a modest fee to review your agreement, assess whether you have any real rights of value you would be releasing, and make recommendations about how best to achieve your goals. It is money well spent. Your lawyer's fee will act as a cheap insurance policy. Your lawyer will examine the release agreement to make sure it does not purport to release more than you intend. In cases in which your employer has accused you of some wrongdoing, your lawyer may take steps to make the release agreement mutual, so that your employer cannot sue you for anything later.

Do not rely on any verbal promises by your employer outside the severance agreement. Unless a promised payment, privilege, or benefit is included in the severance agreement, you may never see it. Those agreements can have *integration clauses* that specify that the terms of the agreement supercede any prior understandings, oral or written. Rules of evidence preclude you from even talking in court about what other verbal promises were made outside that agreement in the face of what purports to be a complete written document on the subject. If the matter is important to you, get it in writing.

Severance Tips List

1. If you do not have a legal case, you may be more effective than a lawyer in negotiating a severance benefit.
2. Use a third party's expert assessment of the likely period of your unemployment as negotiating leverage.
3. Do not sign a severance agreement that contains a release of liability in favor of your employer without consulting with a lawyer.
4. In addition to the amount of severance, be sure to consider other economic terms, such as:
    + lump sum or installments;
    + continuation of fringe benefits;
    + a statement of any other monies to be paid or property to be transferred to you; and,
    + outplacement services.
5. Consider noneconomic terms, such as:
    + nondisparagement clause;
    + letter of recommendation;
    + procedure for responding to third party inquiries; and,
    + agreement not to contest your application for unemployment benefits.
6. Consult with a lawyer to ensure:
    + you are not releasing valuable employment claims;
    + you are not releasing vested rights;
    + the agreement does not overreach with respect to non-compete, penalty, or litigation clauses; and,
    + the agreement contains special provisions you may need, such as a mutual release or an indemnity and hold harmless agreement.

Chapter 10

All About Lawyers

Not long after being terminated, you will recover from the initial shock. You will then begin to feel anger that your former employer has taken away your means of supporting yourself and your family. It is only natural that one of the things you will begin to consider is whether your former employer can be sued for taking that away. It may be that the reason for the termination—or how it was handled—makes it unlawful. The existence of an element of unlawful conduct in your termination can create legal rights you can use to obtain compensation for the damage that unlawful termination caused. As those legal rights may have substantial value, it would be prudent to have a competent professional assess whether and to what extent such value exists. In order to obtain an accurate assessment of that value, it is important to select the right lawyer.

How to Find a Lawyer

The most important decision you make in the quest to vindicate your legal rights is your selection of a lawyer. There are widely varying skill and experience levels of people who practice employment law. Do not expect that finding the right attorney for you will be easy. When you start your search, you may feel bounced around by the lawyers you call. You may become frustrated because some may not call you back. Be patient, persistent, and methodical. This will be one of the most important activities you will undertake after your termination.

There are various sources to help you find an attorney. The names of attorneys who practice employment law may be secured through the *lawyer referral service* run by most state bar associations. However, that is not always the best resource. That list is made up of attorneys who choose to participate in the service. Each attorney is allowed to designate the types of cases he or she chooses to have referred. Typically, there is no screening process to make sure the attorney is experienced in any particular legal area. Most experienced employment attorneys do not rely upon such services for a substantial part of their referral base. Many young lawyers sign up to be listed in those services for lack of better referral sources.

Private referral services are also available. In recent years, companies have been formed that advertise themselves to the public as lawyer referral services. In reality, they only give out the names of lawyers who are willing to pay a fee for inclusion on their referral panel. There is no assurance that the attorneys who sign up with such referral services are the best in the field. Similarly, with Yellow Page advertisements there is absolutely no screening process that controls the claims made in those ads.

By far the best way to find a good employment lawyer is by *personal referral*. Family, friends, or co-workers may have had a good experience with an employment lawyer. Better still, call a lawyer, either an employment lawyer who practices on the defense side or a lawyer outside that area of specialty who has been around for awhile, and ask that lawyer for a referral to a plaintiff's employment specialist. The lawyer you talk to will take care to give you a referral to a good lawyer. Otherwise, he or she could be responsible for a negligent referral. That is great motivation to a lawyer.

The lawyer may refer you to more than one employment attorney. If the lawyer gives you several names, ask the lawyer who he or she would recommend if it were for a family member.

There are also a few reliable lawyer rating services. Two good references that are available are the *Martindale-Hubbell* legal directory and the publication *The Best Lawyers in America*. Those sources are based upon peer ratings. A lawyer cannot purchase—or even influence—their rating in those publications. It is based on the quality of work they produce.

Martindale-Hubbell relies on the opinions of lawyers in the community. It rates lawyers by quality ("a" or "b") and integrity ("v" is for very high). Look for an "av" attorney or firm. That directory is available online at **www.martindale.com**.

The *Best Lawyers in America* is also based on local peer ratings, but from specialists in the field. One field of specialty that is rated is *labor and employment law*. Lawyers who represent employees are listed for each of the fifty states. The *Best Lawyers* listings are available online at **www.bestlawyers.com** for a subscription fee of $100. Hardbound volumes of that publication may be available in your local library. In the hardbound volumes, look for an employment specialist who represents *individuals*. However, if you mistakenly contact a management lawyer, ask that person who they respect most for the plaintiff's side in town. They are usually not hesitant about letting inquirers know that.

Engaging Your Lawyer

Once you have located the right lawyer, you need to make personal contact with that lawyer to see if he or she is someone in whom you can invest your confidence.

THE INITIAL MEETING WITH THE LAWYER

The most important thing to know about dealing with lawyers is that they are people, too. Some are even nice people. Typically, before you have seen your lawyer, you have spoken with him or her and passed a telephone screening. The lawyer who has agreed to meet with you in person thinks there may be some value to your case. In the employment field, only one in about twenty people have a case. So you should feel good that yours has passed the first screening stage.

The point is, the lawyer who meets with you is just as hopeful as you that things will work out in the interview. Their agenda is not to defeat your case. That being so, relax in the interview and be yourself. Be natural and genuine, but keep your emotions in check. If you become too emotional during the interview, your lawyer may have to terminate it altogether because he or she cannot get you to calmly respond to the questions that need to be answered in order to give your case careful evaluation.

The next most important thing to know is that while you may think you know what is important to tell your lawyer, you do not. Experienced employment lawyers know that if they let you just start talking about your case, they will never get to the heart of it. You have biases and defense mechanisms just like everyone else. Over time, you may have constructed a story about what happened that is inadvertently shaded with bias that favors you and omits unfavorable information that you would rather not have others hear, at least initially.

Because experienced employment lawyers know this, they will usually not let you just tell your story. Instead, they will ask you questions, starting with most recent events. This method may not be what you were expecting. Do not fight it. It is the best way to get to the truth, so as to be able to evaluate your case. You certainly do not want to be quarrelsome with your lawyer in the initial interview. That may influence the lawyer not to take your case. He or she would rather lose the fee than have to deal with a difficult client for the next year or two.

You can be sure the lawyer will ask:

+ when you were terminated and by whom;
+ if that person was your supervisor and for how long;
+ what the stated reason for termination was; and,
+ what you believe the real reason for termination was and why.

You will be asked all sorts of questions to test the validity of your responses.

Engage in full disclosure. Reveal not only facts that are helpful to you, but those that are harmful as well. An opinion from an attorney that is based on incomplete information is worse than useless—it is misleading. Do not do yourself the disservice of causing your lawyer to draw you into litigation because you gave inaccurate information that artificially inflated your attorney's evaluation of the prospects of your case.

If you started a narrative of events before termination, your attorney will ask you to bring it up to date and provide it. Your attorney may also ask you for a list of names, addresses, and telephone numbers of witnesses who know something about your case. You may be asked by your attorney to help in the scheduling of witness interviews, by contacting those people first and letting them know your lawyer will be speaking with them.

At the end of the interview, your attorney should have a pretty good idea whether you have a case, based on the information provided. In some cases, the lawyer may even be able to place a percentage probability of success on the case. In other cases, more information may need to be gathered before the lawyer can do so. That information may take the form of additional documents, including your personnel file. It may take speaking with witnesses.

At some point, however, once your attorney stops asking for information, it is fair for you to ask the lawyer to commit. Do not be afraid to ask questions like the following.

+ "Do you think I have a case?"
+ "What is the likelihood we will succeed?"
+ "What do you think it is worth?"

Listen to the answers carefully. Ask the lawyer to explain why he or she feels the way he or she does. Evaluate whether the answers to those questions make sense to you.

Also, do not be afraid to ask the lawyer how long he or she has been practicing law, and more particularly, employment law. Ask how long he or she has been with the firm and what kind of support staff is available to help on your case. Observe the office and judge whether you feel comfortable in those surroundings. Look at any plaques that are on display that advertise the education or the accomplishments of the lawyer.

Each lawyer has a different style. There are many different styles that are effective. You find that competent lawyers come in all sorts of flavors. There are some lawyers who are quite effective even though they do not appear to be a *barracuda*. A lawyer can be assertive in pursuing your interests and still be reasonable. In fact, a lawyer who is overly aggressive can work against you. If they appear so in the tone of a letter to your employer while you are employed, your employer could resent that and take that out on you and fire you for it. If the lawyer angers your opponent's lawyer during litigation by engaging in sharp or underhanded tactics, settlement could be impeded. You do not want a lawyer who gets your opponent personally invested in defeating you.

Nor do you want your opponent to be able to relate to a jury how they tried to work with you to save your employment, but your lawyer's unreasonable demands or behavior made that impossible.

Juries do not like lawyers. They also do not like employees who would *sic* a rabid lawyer on an employer. You want an effective, competent lawyer, who may be aggressive—but not unreasonably so.

If you decide you like the lawyer and feel confident with him or her, you are at the stage in which you can discuss fees and enter into an agreement to formally *retain* that lawyer to represent you in your case.

FEES

There are two basic ways to hire a lawyer—pay an *hourly rate* or hire him or her on a *contingent* basis. The contingency fee will equal a percentage of what the lawyer recovers for you.

Whether to propose to the lawyer to be paid hourly or on a contingent basis largely depends on the services you wish the lawyer to perform. If you want the lawyer to just write a demand letter, an hourly fee is probably more appropriate. It would be a good idea for you to ask the lawyer *not to exceed* a particular figure without your further authority. Most good lawyers have a pretty good idea how much time will be required to render a particular service and will be willing to put a cap on it in that way.

However, in most cases, the services you will want the lawyer to provide will be to recover a substantial amount for you because of lost income due to a wrongful termination. Many hours will need to be invested by the lawyer in building and creating value in your case. It is not unusual for several hundred hours to be expended doing that. This is why, in most cases, you will be looking to find someone who is willing to work on a contingent basis.

On a contingent fee basis, if nothing is recovered, you will owe your lawyer nothing, except the out-of-pocket costs your lawyer has expended for filing fees, depositions, and other direct litigation expenses. Typically, those expenses range between $1,500-$4,000 in individual cases. The amount depends on:

+ the size of the employer;
+ the number of depositions that need to be taken and sub-poenas issued; and,
+ whether an expert witness, such as a doctor, economist, or vocational counselor, must be retained.

That may sound like a lot of money, but for every dollar in costs you incur, you will be looking for many times that amount in return for your investment. Also, keep in mind that your lawyer will be expending ten, twenty, or sometimes even fifty times that amount in the value of his or her time fighting to advance your interests.

Retainer Agreements

Most lawyers will have you sign a formal *retainer agreement*. That agreement will contain the terms of your lawyer's hiring. It will state the basis for compensation for the lawyer and your payment obligations for court filing fees and litigation expenses. It may contain some conditions that if they occur, would justify your lawyer's withdrawal from the case. It may also contain provisions making you liable for payment of costs and for some fees in the event you change attorneys.

There is not a lot of regulation restricting the content of such agreements, so there is no such thing as a *standard* agreement. Typically, their content is driven by the personal experiences of the lawyer drafting them. Read it carefully. Take it home before sign-ing it if you have any questions about it. Attempt to negotiate out or clarify any objectionable or troublesome clauses. If you have a good case, you have some negotiating leverage.

Chapter 11

Unlawful Terminations

Most terminations, no matter how unfair, are perfectly legal. There are three basic ways in which a termination can be unlawful:

1. if the termination violates the *public policy* of the state in which it occurred, so that under that state's tort law, the courts of that state permit the employee to sue for common law *wrongful discharge*;

2. if the termination violates a federal or state discrimination, retaliation, or whistleblowing *statute*; or,

3. if the termination violates an *enforceable promise* between the employer and the employee as a matter of contract law.

Public Policy Wrongful Discharge

In all states but Montana, the general rule of at-will employment prevails. Again, at-will employment means the employee may be terminated for any reason or no reason at all, unless the circumstances of the termination fall within an exception to the rule.

Since 1975, the great majority of states have accepted common law *wrongful discharge* as one of those exceptions—but only under limited circumstances. In most cases, in order to assert a wrongful discharge claim, an employee has to show that he or she was terminated contrary to *public policy*. Typically, this requires the employee to prove they were terminated for engaging in conduct that is so important, as reflected in constitutional provisions, statutes, and regulations, that a state considers that conduct *protected activity*. In other words, conduct that, unless protected from termination, would cause an important state policy to be sacrificed.

In most states, the claim will lie only if the termination was in *retaliation* for the employee's conduct. In a few states—including Delaware, Maryland, Vermont, Virginia, and the District of Columbia—the courts have said that a purely discriminatory discharge is equally contrary to public policy. Discriminatory discharge is one in which the person is terminated because of their *protected class status* (race, age, sex, etc.). Those states allow the claim without proof the termination was in retaliation for the employee's conduct.

In all states that have recognized the tort of wrongful discharge, there must be a *public* rather than a *private* interest that is implicated by the termination. Therefore, an individual terminated for acting to protect his or her own personal interest cannot bring the claim. As each case is presented for decision, the court's concern is whether a public policy will be thwarted if legal protection is not afforded.

The tort of wrongful discharge is in its infancy by historical standards. Even today it has not been universally accepted in the United States. Georgia has thus far refused to recognize it, citing traditional adherence to the rule of at-will employment. Florida has refused to recognize it, apart from one case in which it begrudgingly acknowledged clear statutory authority to bring it. In a few other states, the tort has remained remarkably underdeveloped.

No standard has been uniformly applied that establishes fixed and predictable categories of activity by employees that will be protected. In most states where the tort is recognized, it has been applied to cases in which an employee has:

+ refused to *engage* in illegal activity;
+ *reported* illegal activity;
+ *performed* a public duty (like reporting to jury duty); or,
+ pursued an employment right or benefit made available by statute, such as filing a workers' compensation claim.

Even within these well-recognized categories, however, there is debate. In reporting illegal activity, for example, some states, including Arkansas, Connecticut, Minnesota, Nevada, New Jersey, Oklahoma, Pennsylvania, Texas, and Utah, appear to require a report to an appropriate law enforcement or regulatory agency outside the employer. However, about the same number of states, including Arizona, California, Connecticut, Illinois, Kansas, Maryland, Massachusetts, and Oregon, afford protection whether or not the report was made internally or outside the employer.

Similarly, most states that have decided the question have held that an employee need not prove the actual unlawfulness of the employer's conduct, just the employee's good faith belief that the conduct was unlawful. In Pennsylvania, though, if the employer's conduct was not in fact illegal, it has been held that the employee has no claim. However, there is universal agreement that an employee who complains of conduct they do not think is unlawful, but just amounts to unwise business practices, may not pursue a wrongful discharge claim. Nor are employees protected in any state who merely complain that the employer has failed to follow its own policies or practices, or has merely failed to make the best business decision. The only exception is when the employer is a government body and a state statute protects persons who engage in whistleblowing activities associated with a public employer's gross mismanagement or waste of public funds.

For a listing of some of the notable and recent wrongful discharge cases that have been decided in each jurisdiction, see Appendix G.

Wrongful Constructive Discharge

Employees frequently ask, "Is it possible to sue my employer if I resign?" It may be that you are about to resign because your employer has been harassing you because of your protected class status or because you have engaged in some kind of protected activity. Most employers believe, rightly or wrongly, that if they terminate someone outright, that employee can more easily make a case out of it than if the employee quits. Therefore, it is often the case that an employer will intentionally engage in harassment for the purpose of attempting to make an employee resign. In the early days of employment law, an employee who resigned under those circumstances was left without a remedy.

As years went by, courts were presented with too many cases in which it would be unjust to leave an employee, whose resignation was intentionally precipitated by the employer because of their protected class status or activity without a remedy. Courts slowly began to fashion new rules to allow for the recovery to employees who resigned, but under very limited circumstances. Federal courts led the way. In interpreting Title VII, they began to allow workers who resigned to pursue a claim for wrongful *constructive* termination, but only where the employee could prove the employer had intentionally created a work atmosphere that was *intolerable.*

Similarly, in most states that have since decided the issue, those courts have held there are some limited circumstances in which employees will be allowed to sue even though they resigned. In those cases, the law will *deem* that a termination has occurred as a fictional legal *construct*—thus, the term *wrongful constructive termination.*

The laws of the states differ as to what those qualifying circumstances are. To discourage fraudulent suits, the standard has invariably been a strict one. In harassment type cases it is typically required that the level of intolerability be *objectively* determined. It usually is expressed as a level of harassment that is so intolerable, no reasonable person would have any alternative but to resign. That means that even though you may *subjectively* feel that your employer's conduct toward you is horrible and that you cannot take it anymore, a judge or jury will be able to *second guess* you later on.

If they believe that you were *hypersensitive* or that you *jumped the gun*, you may lose the case, because you will be unable to prove the employer was legally responsible for your resignation. It is important to keep in mind, though, that harassment generally is not illegal. You can prove you were subjected to the most egregious harassment possible and be left without a remedy if you resign, unless you prove the employer engaged in that conduct because of your protected class status or because you had engaged in protected activity.

State Statutory Solutions

Some jurisdictions regulate wrongful discharge by statute. In Montana, state law requires an employer to have good cause to terminate a worker who has passed their probationary period, which, if not defined by the employer, is six months. As the *quid pro quo* for that employment security, in Montana there is no tort of wrongful discharge. No other state has followed suit.

On the other hand, some states have adopted legislation to narrow or define the tort of wrongful discharge. Nebraska, for example, has specified by statute the categories of public policy exceptions to at-will employment it will accept in a wrongful discharge claim. Arizona and Virginia have passed similar legislation.

Discrimination Laws

Many discrimination laws that prohibit a discriminatory termination have been enacted by both Congress and many of the state legislatures. In 1964, Congress passed the *Civil Rights Act*. Title VII of the Act prohibits discrimination in the now familiar categories of race, color, religion, sex, and national origin. That legislation bars discrimination in terms, conditions, and privileges of employment, including termination of employees.

In 1967, Congress passed the *Age Discrimination in Employment Act* (ADEA) to prohibit age discrimination. The ADEA was followed in 1972 by the *Rehabilitation Act*. It prohibits discrimination against disabled persons by government employers and certain federal contractors. Those acts were followed by the passage of the *Americans with Disabilities Act of 1990* (ADA) and the *Family and Medical Leave Act* (FMLA) three years afterwards. Various state legislatures followed Congress' lead, and in the last forty years adopted a wide variety of statutes prohibiting discrimination.

The following is a list of the principal federal statutes that protect you from a discriminatory termination.

- *Title VII of the Civil Rights Act of 1964*—prohibits *discrimination* with respect to race, color, national origin, sex, and religion.
- *The Civil Rights Act of 1870*—passed in the post-Civil War Reconstruction era, but not used as an effective tool by terminated employees until after the passage of Title VII. Provides more extensive remedies than Title VII for *intentional discrimination based on race*.
- *Age Discrimination in Employment Act of 1967* (ADEA)—prohibits discrimination in employment against any person 40 years of age and over *because of their age*.

+ *Americans with Disabilities Act of 1990* (ADA)—prohibits discrimination against a *disabled person* who can perform the essential functions of his or her position with or without reasonable accommodation on the basis of an actual or perceived physical or mental impairment.
+ The *Family and Medical Leave Act*—prohibits discrimination against employees who take *family leave.*

Millions of people are protected by the wide swath of this legislation. Title VII applies to employers having as few as fifteen employees. It has been construed to prohibit all racial discrimination in employment, including against Caucasians. Its proscription against national origin discrimination has been held to apply whether or not the victim is a citizen of the United States. It also prohibits discrimination against persons because of their association with a person of a racial group or foreign national origin. Sex discrimination includes discrimination on the basis of pregnancy and sexual harassment. Recent cases give protection to homosexuals in some situations, when they are the victim of sex-specific conduct, when the harasser displays a hostility towards workers of a particular sex in the workplace, or when they are terminated because they did not meet their employer's stereotyped expectations of their sex. Title VII not only prohibits discrimination on the basis of religious belief, observance, and practice, but also requires employers to reasonably accommodate those practices unless the employer demonstrates it would be an undue hardship on its business.

The Americans with Disabilities Act, which also applies to employers having fifteen or more employees, protects persons from discrimination with respect to both actual or perceived physical or mental impairments. It does not protect disabled persons from termination who cannot do the work in question. It protects only those who can, with or without *reasonable accommodation.* It places a burden on employers to reasonably accommodate disabled persons, unless that would constitute an undue hardship. Accommodation can take many forms, including providing access to work stations, job modification, equipment modification, or reassignment. What a reasonable accommodation is depends on the facts of each case. Factors looked at include:

+ the size of the employer;
+ the cost of the accommodation; and,
+ the impact of the accommodation on the operation of the facility.

STATE LAWS

Because federal discrimination law only applies to employers of a certain size, private employers in those states with under fifteen employees are not regulated against termination on the basis of race, color, sex, religion, or national origin. Therefore, almost all states have passed some form of statewide discrimination statute that bars a discriminatory termination. However, the scope of those statutes differ wildly. For example, Alabama only prohibits discrimination on the basis of age. Mississippi's discrimination laws regulate public sector, but not private sector employment.

In addition to the categories protected under federal law, many state statutes also prohibit discrimination based on *marital status* or change in marital status. Many also provide statutory protection against retaliation for filing a state civil rights or workers' compensation claim. Persons who serve in the state military are typically given state statutory protection. Eighteen states have created *ancestry* as a protected class, in addition to *national origin*. Those two categories together would protect against discrimination if you or your parents were born in a foreign country. Vermont's even broader statute, which prohibits discrimination based upon *place of birth*, bans discrimination against persons born domestically in other states. Eight states have included *creed* as a separate category in addition to *religion*, to broaden protection based upon one's beliefs.

Not all state statutes that prohibit other forms of discrimination outlaw disability discrimination. On the other hand, some states have broader statutory disability protection than under federal law. Washington state bars physical, mental, and *sensory* disability discrimination. New Mexico extends its health-related protection against discrimination to persons with *serious medical conditions*. California protects against discrimination based on a *medical condition*, which it restrictively defines as relating to a history of cancer or genetic characteristic. Hawaii and Oregon extend legal protection to employees who are *associated with* a disabled person, to reach situations in which an employer may think itself burdened by the cost or distraction associated with an employee's disabled dependent.

Age discrimination, likewise, is given widely differing treatment by the states. Some states follow the age 40 and over federal standard before offering protection. Very few states, including Minnesota, New Jersey, and Oregon, have adopted statutes that recognize that there are some situations in which an employee may experience discrimination because he or she is too young. Those states provide legal protection against age discrimination to all employees who have attained majority.

While there is no federal law banning *sexual orientation* discrimination in the private sector, thirteen states and the District of Columbia have made sexual orientation discrimination by private employers unlawful by state statute. Those states are:

+ California
+ Connecticut
+ Hawaii
+ Maryland

- ✦ Massachusetts
- ✦ Minnesota
- ✦ Nevada
- ✦ New Hampshire
- ✦ New Jersey
- ✦ New Mexico
- ✦ Rhode Island
- ✦ Vermont
- ✦ Wisconsin

Another half dozen—Illinois, Indiana, New York, Ohio, Pennsylvania, and Washington—prohibit such discrimination in public employment.

Pro-family legislation has created even more protected classes at the state level. A handful of states and the District of Columbia prohibit *family relationship* discrimination of one form or another. This is to prohibit termination because a family member works or used to work for the employer. Alaska prohibits *parenthood* discrimination. The District of Columbia has taken it a step further and prohibits discrimination against persons who have discharged *family responsibilities,* which its law leaves undefined. Mothers who *breast-feed* or express milk at work are protected in Hawaii, Minnesota, New Mexico, Oregon, and Tennessee. In North Carolina, an employer cannot discriminate against an employee for participating in *court-ordered parental duties* or for taking up to four hours' leave per year to attend activities at a child's school.

Privacy concerns have stimulated still other local legislation. Five states bar discrimination against persons who have lawfully used lawful products off the employer's premises during non-working hours. A few others specifically protect persons who lawfully use tobacco. Minnesota prohibits discrimination against employees who fail to contribute to *charity*.

In addition to those statutes aimed to protect private activity, other statutes protect private information. Seven states now prohibit discrimination on the basis of *genetic information* or condition. One state, New Jersey, outlaws such discrimination for atypical cellular or blood trait. Three states make it illegal to discriminate against someone who has received *public assistance*. Two states prohibit discrimination on the basis of one's *criminal history*. Massachusetts prohibits discrimination on the basis of a person's *mental commitment history*.

Two jurisdictions regulate discrimination purely on *physical characteristics*. Michigan bans discrimination based on *height or weight*. The District of Columbia, creating probably the most wide sweeping of all protected class categories, bans discrimination based on *personal appearance*.

The number of employees in the employer's workforce required to activate the legal protection afforded by a state discrimination statute also differs from state to state. For example, in Missouri the employer must have at least six employees. In Virginia, the employer is regulated only if it has between five and fifteen employees. In Oregon, the number is six for disability discrimination, but one in most other cases.

For a detailed listing of the notable discrimination statutes in each state, and contact information for the state civil rights enforcement agency in each state that has one, see Appendix D.

Opposition and Retaliation Statutes

In addition to the many statutory proscriptions against unlawful discrimination, federal and state statutes prohibit retaliatory termination under certain circumstances. Many of those statutes provide protection for those who report or oppose unlawful discrimination. Other special legislation prohibits the termination of *whistleblowers*—those who report illegal activity—in some cases.

OPPOSITION STATUTES

All of the major federal laws that protect employees against discrimination, including *Title VII* of the *1964 Civil Rights Act*, the *Age Discrimination in Employment Act*, the *Americans with Disabilities Act*, and the *Family and Medical Leave Act*, bar retaliation against employees who report or oppose unlawful discrimination. *Opposition statutes* essentially are whistleblowing statutes that apply in the discrimination context. However, they have broader applicability because they protect not only the original victims of discrimination, but also those who are witnesses on the victims' behalf.

WHISTLEBLOWING STATUTES

Other federal laws afford legal protection from termination to employees who report other kinds of illegal activity. The *Occupational Safety and Health Act* (OSHA) bars retaliation against a person who has made a complaint about health or safety with the employer or with OSHA. The federal *Whistleblower Protection Act* applies only to employees of the federal government. It bars retaliation against federal employees who report unlawful activity, gross management, a gross waste of funds, abuse of authority, or *substantial or specific* damages to public health and safety. Federal law also protects whistleblowers who file claims on behalf of the federal government for fraud against federal contractors under the *False Claims Act* from retaliation.

A host of other federal statutes protect persons from a retaliatory termination who have engaged in whistleblowing activities. Those activities include reports of violations of federal laws that regulate the environment (such as the *Clean Air Act*), that regulate employee health (such as the *Coal Mine Health and Safety Act*), or that regulate public safety (such as the *Toxic Substances Control Act*).

Most recently, in the aftermath of the Enron scandal, Congress passed the *Sarbanes-Oxley Act*. It demands greater corporate accountability for financial reporting, and includes whistleblower protection from a retaliatory termination. This protection is for employees who provide information about acts they reasonably believe to be in violation of the rules of the Securities and Exchange Commission or any law relating to fraud against shareholders. Protection is expansively given under the Act. Employees are protected from retaliation not only where they provide information to a federal regulatory or law enforcement agency, but also to an employee of the corporation whose job it is to stop such behavior or even to their own supervisor.

STATUTES RELATING TO OTHER PROTECTED ACTIVITIES

Other federal statutes prohibit a termination for engaging in protected activities other than whistleblowing, such as for reporting for military service (pursuant to the *Uniformed Services Employment and Reemployment Rights Act* (USERRA)), or for reporting for federal jury duty. The *National Labor Relations Act* bars retaliation against a person who engages in union activity. The *Fair Labor Standards Act* bars retaliation against a person who makes a wage claim under that statute.

STATE WHISTLEBLOWING LAWS

Many states have whistleblowing laws of their own. Many have opposition statutes that prohibit a retaliatory termination for reporting or opposing discrimination. Many also have other anti-retaliation provisions for engaging in various forms of activity the states have encouraged. For example, sixteen states have a statute that bars retaliation for filing a workers' compensation claim. About a dozen states have a statute that bars retaliation for taking family leave. Connecticut bars an employer from retaliating against an employee who exercises his or her free speech rights under the United States or Connecticut Constitutions, with limited exceptions.

Many states have also adopted statutes that protect persons from a retaliatory termination who have reported various forms of illegal activity. However, just as courts have differed from state to state as to the details of such protection, so too have the legislatures in the several states similarly differed. They differ as to the gravity of the offense that is being reported. Misconduct that does not rise to the level of a violation of law, gross mismanagement, or abuse of authority is typically not covered.

They also differ in their requirement of whether conduct being reported is actually illegal. For example, to afford protection against retaliation, Iowa requires only a reasonable belief that the conduct was unlawful. New York, on the other hand, affords no protection for reporting what was thought by an employee to be illegal activity unless an actual violation of law occurred. In the same vein, some statutes, including those in Florida and Texas, afford protection only if the whistleblower makes his or her report to a government agency.

The statutes of other states, like that in Kansas, provide protection even in cases of internal reports to the employer. In Maine and New York, no protection is afforded unless the whistleblower first gives the employer a chance to remedy the situation. Some state whistleblower statutes protect government workers, but not private employees.

Employment Contracts

In the last quarter century, courts have recognized that employment, even at-will employment, is essentially *contractual* in nature. Today, the courts in most states accept that promises made by at-will employers to their employees are as entitled to legal enforcement as any other promises they make. Further, they have recognized that, as in most other settings, agreements can arise *expressly* or by *implication*. If you and your employer agree, for example, that the terms of a progressive discipline policy contained in an employee handbook will govern your employment, that is an express agreement. If, on the other hand, nothing is expressly stated to that effect, but the handbook containing such a policy is given to you to read and follow, the courts in most states have recognized that under those circumstances, an enforceable contract is implied. Your employer impliedly agreed that it is bound by the handbook as well. In either case, in most states if the employer breaches that promise, it can be held accountable for breach of contract if it terminates you contrary to the terms of that promise.

Enforceable promises contained in employee handbooks can take many forms, such as:

+ promises of *fair* treatment;
+ promises of *warnings* before termination;
+ promises of *progressive discipline*; and,
+ a promise you may exercise its *open door* policy.

As courts held statements made in handbooks by employers as enforceable promises, lawyers for employers began to couch handbook language in softer, less definite language of intention, such as, "Ordinarily we will follow this procedure." Attorneys for employers then began to insert what became known as contract *disclaimers* at the beginning of each employee handbook. The disclosures said that the handbook was not an employment contract, that nothing in the handbook was intended as a promise, and that the relationship between the employer and its employees was *at will*.

In addition, employers began to require employees to sign acknowledgments that they read and understood the handbook provisions, including those disclaimers. Despite the disparity in power between the parties, and the lack of any real opportunity to negotiate the terms of employment by employees, most courts give effect to those disclaimers.

However, contract liability has continued to be generated in the course of employee terminations. First, not all promises made by employers are in the form of a handbook. During pre-hire negotiations, for example, there is no way to innoculate an employer from liability with a disclaimer, because so much of the interaction between the employer and the prospective employee is verbal. Representations relating to compensation, title, or job security during the recruitment phase have continued to serve as a hotbed for litigation. Similarly, during post-hire employee orientation, questions prompted by handbook provisions generate verbal and written responses that are themselves outside the shroud of a protective disclaimer.

Further, after employment commences, internal memoranda that carry language of promise that are distributed to employees frequently do not contain a disclaimer. Verbal promises by supervisors during one-on-ones with the employee also do not contain disclaimers. In such cases, most courts will hold that the at-will employment relationship can be *modified* by a subsequent written or verbal understanding.

Finally, some courts have taken the position that the relationship between the parties can be modified, based not upon any single statement that would be susceptible to a disclaimer, but upon the parties' entire *course of dealing*. Many courts will examine all of the facts and circumstances to determine if the at-will relationship has been modified by the *past practices* of the parties. In those cases, the courts will look to things such as the employee handbook, company policy, and oral representations. *Routine practice* can serve as the foundation for an implied contract claim, despite the existence of a disclaimer in the employee handbook.

Some employees have successfully asserted that, because of the dealings between the parties, the at-will aspect of the relationship is modified so that employment can only be terminated at or after a particular time. In other cases, the courts have held that promises about the conditions under which the employee was first hired may limit the ability of the employer to terminate at will. Thus, statements regarding assurances of employment *as long as we have production to run*, may be a promise of a job as long as the work the employee was able to do was needed. Other courts have enforced assurances of security as a promise of permanent employment. In one case, a contract for permanent employment was enforced based upon a promise that if the employee accepted employment, he *would spend the rest of his working career* with that employer.

Still other courts have found employers precluded by their promises from terminating an employee because of the happening of some event. In one case, a court held that where a company president told the employee to "take all the time he needed" to recover from his illness, and he did, the company breached an implied contract arising from that statement when it terminated him for absenteeism.

Chapter 12

Other Legal Claims

Sometimes a termination does not fall within one of the exceptions to at-will employment. However, the manner in which the employer acted during the employment relationship or in the course of termination may create a separate right to bring a legal claim against the employer.

If your supervisor has made false and malicious statements about you to cause your termination because of some personal vendetta, that may entitle you to sue for defamation. If the publication has been to a sufficiently large number of people, that may allow you to sue for invasion of privacy for presenting you in a false light in the public eye. If the tactics used to force you out have been sufficiently outrageous, you may be able to bring a claim for intentional infliction of severe emotional distress. If, in the process of forcing you out, it becomes apparent the employer never intended to comply with its promises to you, you may have an action for fraud.

Finally, if the company itself has no assets with which to pay a judgment, but you prove the firing manager—who does have sufficient assets—acted by improper means or for an improper purpose, you may be able to sue the manager personally to recoup your loss.

Other legal claims a lawyer may be able to assert on your behalf if you are terminated are:

+ intentional infliction of severe emotional distress (sometimes known as outrageous conduct);
+ intentional interference with economic relations;
+ invasion of privacy;
+ defamation; and,
+ misrepresentation.

Intentional Infliction of Severe Emotional Distress

Sometimes an event is so far outside the bounds of acceptable conduct that it can be fairly categorized as *outrageous*. In some states, this type of event has been recognized as the tort of *intentional infliction of emotional distress*. Generally, where it has been recognized, you must show:

+ that the employer either acted *intentionally* to cause you to suffer emotional distress or acted in reckless disregard of the probability you would suffer such distress;
+ that the conduct is so far outside the bounds of accepted conduct it is outrageous; and,
+ that the conduct has resulted in *severe* emotional or mental distress.

This tort is sort of a *catchall* for highly unusual cases that defy categorization. Because it lacks definition, its utilization is frequently attempted. For both of those reasons it is not favored in the courts. Most trial judges require extreme facts before they will allow this claim to proceed to trial. It is sometimes said that the facts have to pass the *Oh, my God!* test. It is often difficult to move an experienced judge to invoke the Almighty. That high bar is intended to prevent people from suing for the mean, rude, or insulting conduct that is merely part of everyday life. The unstated fear is that without this requirement of a showing of outrageousness, the courts would be overburdened with such suits.

Just as there is no limit to the ways in which an employer could conceivably be abusive, there is no one type of case in which the tort applies. It has frequently been applied in cases involving abusive investigations, shocking behavior, highly offensive physical contact, highly unusual and extreme forms of retaliation, and horrendous treatment of the infirm. Ordinary workplace harassment that does not contain those elements will not qualify.

This tort is relatively new and its application to employment cases is particularly recent. No one can tell its limits at this point. However, in the past few years it has been applied in the following cases:

 + retaliation for reporting sexual harassment;
 + abusive investigations, particularly ones that include false accusations, threats of criminal prosecution, or *gestapo*-type tactics; and,
 + when the employer circulates false rumors of stealing in an effort to force an employee to resign.

As can be seen, the nature of the conduct matters. Unlawful sexual or racial harassment will more likely be the type of conduct the courts will find sufficiently egregious, as opposed to abusive conduct generally. The frequency, duration, and severity of the conduct will also be considered.

Intentional Interference with Economic Relations

In the commercial context, if a competitor of a company uses unfair competition to injure that company's relationship with its customer, it can sue its competitor for tortious third-party interference with economic relations. Similarly, in their quest to find additional remedies, lawyers for terminated employees have attempted to apply the same principle to the workplace. The idea is that if a manager lies about an employee's performance to get him or her fired, why should the employee not be able to sue the manager? Moreover, since the manager was performing his or her duties as a manager at the time (which the law calls acting *within the scope* of employment), why should the employee not be able to sue the company the manager was serving at the time as well? These attempts have been met with mixed success. Some jurisdictions have allowed the employee to sue the manager individually, but only when the manager is acting for his or her own purposes (*i.e.*, outside the scope of employment). Very few have allowed the employee to sue both the manager and the company.

There are some cases in which it makes sense to consider holding the individual actor liable. For example, it may make sense to do so if the corporation itself has no assets or is in bankruptcy, but its president (who fired you) is wealthy.

In most states, to state a claim for intentional interference with economic relations, the employee must prove:

+ the existence of a business relationship;
+ intentional interference with that relationship by a third party, accomplished through improper means or for an improper purpose; and,
+ that interference caused damage.

It is not enough for the employee to prove that the CEO acted solely for his or her own purposes. Those acts also must be proven to be *improper* under the law of that state for the claim to lie, either by proof the CEO acted by *improper means* or for an *improper purpose*. Cases in which this tort has been applied have included the following situations.

+ Where a supervisor induced an employee's termination by saying she was *dissatisfied with her employer and the department,* when that statement was knowingly false.

+ Where a president terminated the employee comptroller in order to force out a major shareholder.

+ Where an employee was terminated soon after she refused the request of a supervisor to submit only some—but not all—files to state authorities, and after her refusal the supervisor threatened to quit if she was not fired.

+ Where an employee was fired by bank officers who induced her termination by making knowingly false and malicious negative statements about her.

+ Where a former employer complained that an employee's hiring was in violation of a noncompete agreement it knew was invalid, causing his termination.

Invasion of Privacy

Under the common law of most states, with the notable exceptions of New York, Minnesota, Louisiana, and Virginia, employees are entitled to protection from unreasonable invasions of privacy. Generally, an invasion of privacy can occur in one of four different ways:

1. *appropriation,* or use, of another's name or likeness without their permission;
2. *unreasonable intrusion* upon the private affairs or seclusion of another;
3. *public disclosure* of private facts; or,
4. placing another in a *false light* in the public eye.

In the employment context, employee privacy rights are most often violated by intrusion into an employee's private affairs or concerns, but employment cases involving all four species of the tort can be found.

INVASION BY INTRUSION

In the great majority of states, an employer that unreasonably intrudes into your private affairs or concerns after you are employed will be liable to you for invasion of privacy. In each case of alleged unlawful intrusion, a balancing test is applied, in which the employee's interest in privacy is weighed against the employer's need to know. To succeed in a claim of invasion of privacy by intrusion, an employee must typically show an *intentional intrusion*—physical or otherwise—upon the employee's *private affairs or concerns* that would be *offensive* to a reasonable person.

There are numerous examples in which the tort has been applied that illustrate how it could be committed in the course of events leading up to a termination:

- ✦ where an employer searched an employee's locker and purse without her permission, and the lock was her property;
- ✦ where the employer allegedly engaged in secret videotaping of employee restrooms through two-way mirrors;
- ✦ where an employee's personal mail at work was opened and read without her authority;
- ✦ where the employer allegedly accessed an employee's home telephone records while investigating the employee's activities during disability leave;
- ✦ where an employer required an employee to take a polygraph exam under threat of losing his job; and,
- ✦ where an employer discussed an employee's confidential medical information with an independent physician it had retained to examine the employee, when permission was required under its own policy to release that information.

Although the tort does not require that you be terminated for a claim to lie, because of the highly charged emotions associated with many terminations, it is not uncommon also to find a violation similar to one of those mentioned.

PUBLIC DISCLOSURE OF PRIVATE FACTS

Sometimes an employer cannot keep the details of a termination quiet. With respect to the species of the tort of invasion of privacy known as *public disclosure of private facts*, which could apply in such a case, the two problematic requirements are that the facts be *private* and that they be *publicly disclosed*. The degree of publicity that is required has given the courts the greatest difficulty. For example, while publication in a newspaper of general circulation is clearly sufficient, disclosure in a private setting to only a small group of co-workers may not be enough. This species of the tort has been applied where:

+ an employee who consulted with her employer's resident nurse concerning a mastectomy she was to undergo learned that the employer released that information to her fellow employees and

+ an employer who wrote to the Army Reserve to verify a former employee's military status and made uncomplimentary statements about the employee in the letter. The statements included that the employee was disloyal, had used his reserve status in an abusive and manipulative manner, and was dismissed because of abandonment of duties and dereliction of supervising responsibilities.

Defamation

For most people who work, their marketability is their most important asset. Nothing bears on one's marketability more than his or her reputation. The law has long recognized that a person has a legal interest in his or her good name. The law of defamation provides a remedy for persons whose reputational interest has been damaged by injurious false communications. A termination provides the principal occasion for the employer to exact that damage.

Not every unkind word is actionable. Only *defamatory communications* give rise to liability. Traditionally, a communication is defamatory if it tends to subject the person to hatred, contempt, or ridicule. It may also be defamatory if it tends to diminish the esteem, respect, goodwill, or confidence in which the person is held by a substantial and respectable minority of the community.

A defamatory communication can be written or oral. At common law, *libel* was based on written communications and *slander* on oral communications. Defamatory television and radio broadcasts are considered to be libel.

Examples of defamatory statements that attended a termination are illustrated in the following cases:

✦ a statement that the employer had strong evidence the employee was involved in a car theft;

✦ a statement by a pastor about a church secretary that charged her with misappropriation of funds at a church meeting;

✦ a statement by a former employer that an employee was discharged, and that he had *questionable loyalty and ethics*;

✦ statement about a microcomputer expert that he had erased computer files; and,

✦ a statement that the employee was terminated for cause.

In order to be actionable, the defamatory communication must be *published* (communicated) to a third person. That means it must be communicated to someone other than the plaintiff employee. It is not actionable if the plaintiff is the only one who hears it. On the other hand, in most states, a communication between employees within the same company is sufficient to satisfy the third party communication requirement. A few states require the publication to be to a person outside the company.

You cannot bring an action for defamation against someone who has merely told the truth about you. The law absolutely permits the circulation of damaging communications about a person, so long as the statements are true. As a statement of opinion is neither true nor false, statements of pure opinion are ordinarily not actionable. This is true unless a person could reasonably conclude they were based on undisclosed facts. Generally, a statement of fact will be considered true if the *gist* of the statement is true, even though the statement contains slight inaccuracies.

Other *privileges* exist in the law to permit defamatory communications. Statements made during *legislative* or *judicial proceedings*, for example, are absolutely protected. Comments made during these proceedings will not subject the speaker to prosecution. However, most other privileges to speak of are not *absolute*, but are *qualified*. These qualified, or conditional, privileges can be lost under some circumstances. For example, your supervisor may be allowed to tell some others in the company what he or she thinks about your performance. When your supervisor does so, he or she is said to be qualifiedly privileged to speak. In that circumstance, he or she can say what he or she thinks about your work, even if the statement is wrong. However, the supervisor must have a *reasonable and good faith belief* that what he or she is saying is true. If not, the privilege is said to be *abused*, and thus lost. If the employer abuses its qualified privilege to speak, the employee wins.

A *qualified privilege* can be lost in any of four different ways:

1. if the speaker does not believe that the statement is true or lacks reasonable grounds to believe it is true;
2. if the statement is made for a purpose other than that for which the privilege is given, as when someone takes the opportunity to speak ill of you when he or she does not have to and are doing it because of a secret personal vendetta;

3. if the statement is made to a person not reasonably believed to be necessary to accomplish the purpose, as when the person broadcasts the defamatory matter to a *broader audience* than necessary to hurt you; and,

4. if the statement includes defamatory matter not reasonably believed to be necessary to accomplish the purpose, as when the supervisor goes out of its way to volunteer derogatory information that does not relate to the discussion at hand.

Cases in which the qualified privilege were lost include ones in which:

+ the employer was reckless in failing to verify the information;
+ the statements were made in anger to prevent future employment;
+ the statements were published without a reasonable belief in order to effectuate the employer's discharge; and,
+ the employee was accused of theft to effectuate his termination when the true reason was related to the cost of his or her industrial injuries.

Misrepresentation

When someone promises you something and then does not fulfill that promise, that is *breach of contract*. When that person knew at the time the promise was made that the promise would not or could not be fulfilled, intending that you act in reliance on that promise anyway, that is *fraud*. In most states, fraud can be based on a representation made with *reckless disregard* as to its truth or falsity. Reckless disregard means having an *I do not care* attitude. In the law of misrepresentation, that means making a promise without knowing whether it can be performed.

An employee who is terminated, particularly if soon after employment, may claim fraud in the recruitment process in connection with the promises made in connection with that recruitment. For example, when a worker is recruited for a position and agrees to take that position, but is never given that position and is soon thereafter terminated, *and* the employer knew at the time the worker was recruited that he or she would not receive the promised position, that is fraud. Similarly, when a worker is intentionally misled about the financial condition of the company and is terminated soon after becoming employed because of its poor financial health, and never would have joined if the true condition had been revealed, that is fraud.

Employees have used misrepresentation as a theory of recovery in cases involving a termination or resignation as follows.

+ Concerning an employee who was tricked into signing a form of resignation, by a representation that if he did not sign, he would be terminated anyway.

+ Concerning an employer's false representation as to how long the employment would last.

+ Concerning a false promise by an employer not to retaliate, to induce an employee to give information about an executive's illegal activity.

+ Concerning an employer's omission to inform a recruit both of its difficulties in developing the system he was hired to work on and of its then existing intention to terminate him if the problems it foresaw came to pass.

+ Concerning an employer's omission to disclose at the time of an employee's hiring that a corporate reorganization was being negotiated that might eliminate his territory.

Misrepresentation has taken an important foothold in employment law. It has only begun to develop as a powerful tool to encourage honest communications in workplace settings.

Chapter 13

Termination of Special Group Members

Union and nonmanagement government workers enjoy legal protection not enjoyed by most other private sector employees. They can only be terminated *for cause*. Although no one's work is perfect, and a highly motivated supervisor can always find some fault with a subordinate's work, these groups are protected from the arbitrary terminations that are motivated by trivial jealousies or personality clashes. In addition, government workers enjoy additional rights because of the constitutional limitations placed on government bodies by the due process and equal protection clauses of the United States Constitution. Government workers also have additional constitutional rights not shared by other workers, including those afforded by the First Amendment guarantee of free speech and free association.

Two groups possess rights not enjoyed by employees at will in the private sector.

Termination of Union Workers

Over the course of the first half of the twentieth century, the organized labor movement significantly altered the right of employers to terminate workers at will. Unions negotiated provisions in collective bargaining agreements that protected members who had passed an initial probationary period from being terminated without *cause, good cause,* or *just cause.* That meant employers were no longer free to terminate employees on a whim, for any or no reason. On the contrary, from that time forward, for a termination of a union member to stand, sufficient grounds had to support it, and its imposition had to stand a test of fundamental fairness.

Today, for a union member to take advantage of that advance and challenge a termination, you must file a timely grievance contesting the termination. Your union shop steward or business agent will be able to assist you in filing the grievance. Contracts differ concerning the amount of time within which to file your grievance. Some grievance filing deadlines can be as short as a few days. Read your contract to know how much time you have to file yours.

Once the grievance is filed, the union and employer typically conduct *step* hearings, in which the parties attempt to resolve the grievance informally at progressively ascending levels of authority. At those step hearings, each side presents its case to the other as to why the termination is or is not justified. If no resolution is reached through the informal step hearings, the union must decide whether your case merits arbitration. Not every case is arbitrated. Courts allow unions to exercise discretion in the determination whether to use their resources to arbitrate a particular case. Legal challenges by employees whose union has refused to arbitrate are sustained only upon a showing that the union's decision was arbitrary, capricious, or in bad faith.

At the arbitration, the person appointed as an arbitrator acts as a judge, takes testimony, and receives documents from each side as in a court of law. This is done under somewhat relaxed rules of evidence. In deciding the case, the arbitrator will consider various factors, such as the seriousness of the offense, whether the offense was repeated, and whether the offender was given all the required warnings that were due. In addition, the arbitrator will consider how the employer has treated incidents of this type in the past, looking for consistency in how similar matters have been handled in the past. The arbitrator has the power to reinstate the employee, with or without backpay, if the arbitrator believes the employee was terminated without just cause.

Because union workers are given special rights through federal legislation, principally the *Labor Management Relations Act* and the *National Labor Relations Act*, courts have held that some of the state law employment claims a worker would otherwise have are *preempted* by the federal law. This happens if their prosecution is *inextricably intertwined* with the terms of a collective bargaining agreement. In other words, if a state law claim calls for the parties to debate the meaning or import of the terms of the collective bargaining agreement, the state law claim cannot be brought.

Do you need your lawyer for the arbitration? In most cases, no. The union will provide a representative for you. In most cases, whether or not the representative is a lawyer, he or she will be more competent and familiar with what it will take to win your case than most of the lawyers you would be able to hire. If, however, you sense that your union representative is lazy, incompetent, or *in bed with* the employer, consider hiring a lawyer for the purpose of looking over your union's shoulder. If properly handled, that could provide extra motivation for your union representative to contact all your witnesses and do the preparation that is required to do a good job for you at the arbitration.

If your union does not properly prepare your case and it can be proven the union acted out of personal hostility toward you, you may be able to sue the union for breach of its duty of fair representation. Again, the Supreme Court has set a high bar for such suits, so mere negligence on the part of the union will ordinarily not suffice. The courts will give wide latitude to the union in deciding how to go about preparing and presenting your case, so long as its presentation is not merely perfunctory. Therefore, in most cases, positive reinforcement by you, and if necessary, your attorney, will serve you better than haranguing the union representative about their work quality or lack of motivation.

Termination of Government Employees

Most government employers grant *for cause* termination protection to their nonmanagement workforce in civil service or merit system personnel rules and regulations. This protection is given whether or not the employees in question are union members. Moreover, once a public employee completes a probationary period and *for cause* protection is bestowed, additional constitutional protections are implicated.

Governmental employees with *for cause* protection are said to have a reasonable expectation of continued employment, and therefore a *property interest* in their job that can only be taken away with *due process*. That right also entitles them to procedural *fundamental fairness* before they may be terminated. Typically, that means they must receive notice of the charges against them and an opportunity to be heard concerning those charges before a termination may lawfully occur. The pretermination hearing that is required may be informal. For example, they may not be entitled to confront and cross-examine witnesses against them, nor must the evidence against them be presented through sworn testimony.

Closely akin to the due process rights of certain public employees, is the *liberty interest* they have in their *good name*. If a government employer in the process of termination falsely accuses an employee of theft, for example, that is said to *stigmatize* his or her reputational interest. In such cases, the public employee is said to be entitled to a *name clearing hearing*. If they are not afforded such a hearing before a termination, they may claim the right to a posttermination hearing or to damages if such a hearing would not right the wrong.

In addition to having property rights in their employment that precludes a termination without due process, government workers are protected from a deprivation of their constitutional rights by the Fourteenth Amendment and the *Civil Rights Act of 1871*. These make persons liable who, acting under *color* of state law, deprives any person of *rights, privileges, or immunities* secured by the constitution. In relation to employment cases, this law has been applied to all types of unlawful discrimination, including cases of race discrimination, sex discrimination, age discrimination, and discrimination on the basis of religion.

The advantage of a Section 1983 claim for the employee in a discrimination case is that there is no administrative process that must be exhausted as there is with *Title VII*, nor does the statute contain a statute of limitations. The courts will look to the most applicable state statute as the limitations period, which will typically be a longer period than under *Title VII*. Therefore, you may still have a claim under Section 1983 to assert even though your *Title VII* rights have expired. The final advantage is that there are no caps on damages under Section 1983, whereas damage limitations apply under *Title VII*.

Further, the First and Fourteenth Amendments to the United States Constitution limit the power of government to limit free speech. Therefore, employees of government bodies have rights unavailable to employees in the private sector. They have the right to speak their mind without pain of retaliation for expressing their grievance. However, not all speech in public sector employment is considered constitutionally protected speech. Rather, such speech is protected only when it addresses a *matter of public concern*. A matter that relates to the political, social, or other concern to the community has been said to be one entitled to constitutional protection. However, speech that relates to the internal workings of a governmental office, even if it complains of unfairness or abusive treatment, may not be deemed protected. In each case, there will be a balancing of interests—the employee's interest in the speech against the employer's interest in maintaining the efficiency of public services.

The results are sometimes unpredictable. The scales have tipped in favor of protection in the following cases:

+ a private complaint to supervisors to protest racially discriminatory school policies;
+ making a safety complaint;
+ a firefighting complaint about budget cuts; and,
+ disclosure of possibly illegal wire taps.

On the other hand, protection was not afforded in the following cases, even though the complaints related to discrimination:

+ a teacher who complained about class size and student discipline;
+ a professor's criticism about the internal process of selecting a university president; and,
+ an employee's complaints about his or her own personal employment conditions.

Government employees are also afforded the freedom to associate with others of their choosing by the First and Fourteenth Amendments. For example, a city may not take action to ban its employees from endorsing political candidates outside of work hours. A public official who is a member of one political party may not retaliate against a public employee because they are a member of a different party.

Chapter 14

Evaluating Your Termination Case

One of the most important decisions you will ever make is whether to file a lawsuit. A critical aspect of that decision relates to your chances of success. Most people have absolutely no idea how to evaluate a case. This chapter is intended to inform you how that is done, so that you can better understand your lawyer's advice and make a more informed decision. Only you can make that decision. It is your case, not your lawyer's.

Evaluating Whether You Have a Case

The most frequently asked question of any plaintiff's attorney is, "Do I have a case?" Two things must work together in your favor to give you a chance of success in a courtroom the facts and the law. Your case must fall within one of the classes for which the law affords a remedy. (Chapters 11, 12, and 13 discussed those classes.) Your facts must also be favorable. This requires an evaluation of the evidence that supports your legal claims. If the reasons stated by your employer for your firing are proved false, this suggests to the jury that you were terminated for some other reason that your employer is not willing to admit. The only credible evidence the jury will be left with is your evidence leading to the conclusion that the termination was unlawful.

Case evaluation is an art, not a science. Some of the factors your attorney would look for in your termination case include:

+ the timing of significant events;
+ whether the linkage between significant events is probable;
+ the absence of other factors that credibly account for the termination;
+ the likelihood the employer would engage in that conduct; and,
+ your believability.

The most important factor is the last. Ultimately, your attorney must *believe in* you. That belief must carry an investment of trust and confidence. Every attorney hopes for a client who is direct, candid, and perceptive, as well as not defensive or vengeful. Lawsuits are not resolved by computers. Rather, they are presented to people. In every lawsuit, the people who decide the case are given two sides to that story. They too must inevitably choose whom to believe. You must be viewed as a good person who intends to tell the truth, no matter what.

The second most important factor in your lawyer's selection process is the nature of the purported *linkage* between significant events. The jury must link the termination to some event. People believe that employers tend to terminate workers who have had an on-the-job injury. Some other linkage factors are not as readily believed. Sometimes a jury must be sensitized to that linkage through expert or anecdotal testimony.

Third, the linkage factor is more powerful if the timing of significant events suggests the connection. A worker who is terminated two days after an on-the-job injury is more likely thought to be terminated for that reason than a worker who is terminated years after an injury, absent complications just prior to the termination.

Lastly, the absence of other factors for the termination must be established. There is always some plausible explanation available for your employer to seize upon to explain why you were lawfully discharged. However, if your employer pointed to a job performance problem as the decisive factor, for example, that explanation would be weakened by proof of disparate treatment, over-scrutinization of work, inadequate warnings, or disproportionate weight given to that problem by your employer.

Case Study:
Fired for Filing a Workers' Compensation Claim

Suppose Bob was doing well at work. Prior to his fall, he received no complaints about his work. But three days after he fell at work and injured his back, and only two days after he filed a workers' compensation claim, he was terminated. The employer contends he was terminated not because of the back injury, but because Bob failed to properly call in to report his absence due to the injury. Bob claims he did call in.

First, the timing of that sequence of events tends to support the view that Bob was terminated either for filing a workers' compensation claim or for sustaining a back injury at work, or both. Second, supervisors are frequently evaluated for salary purposes in part on their safety performance. They are often hostile to workers who file such claims. If evidence of that were present here, that would strengthen the relationship between the termination and the claim filing. Because Bob had no other complaints about his work, no pre-injury performance problem accounts for that linkage. If other injured workers had been terminated in the past under suspicious circumstances, that would further strengthen the case. If there was evidence Bob's supervisor had threatened persons on his shift not to file such claims, that would likewise aid Bob's case. Finally, if Bob can prove he called in or if other non-injured workers had failed to call in, but were not terminated, that differential treatment would tend to disprove the employer's stated reason for termination.

If you think you were fired for filing a workers' compensation claim, the following additional considerations would come into play in assessing the strength of your case.

+ What was your employment history before you filed the claim?

+ How soon were you fired after you filed the claim?

+ How has your employer treated other workers who had filed such claims?

+ Did your employer freely provide you with the appropriate forms to file such a claim?

+ Did your employer make any negative comments when you said you were going to file the claim?

+ Did your employer treat you worse after you filed the claim?

+ Did your performance appraisals change for the worse after your claim was filed?

+ Was your work overscrutinized after the claim was filed?

+ Did you receive any unmerited discipline after the claim was filed?

+ Had you or anyone else been disciplined for the same offense before you filed the claim?

+ Were any job duties taken away from you that you were able to perform after you filed the claim?

+ Were any expected promotions or pay increases taken away after you filed the claim?

+ Were you given light-duty work that was available when your doctor released you for light-duty work?

+ Did your employer become impatient with you about the amount of time you spent on light duty?

+ What amount of medical bills did you incur before returning to work?

+ Did your employer return you to your old job when your doctor released you back to regular work?

+ Were you reinjured after returning to your old job?

+ Is your employer insured or self-insured for such claims?

+ What is your employer's claim history?

+ Is your employer paying an insurance premium that is higher than normal because of its claims history?

+ Is management under pressure to reduce the number and cost of such claims?

+ Has your boss been singled out by management as having had too many such claims?

+ What reasons were given for your termination?

+ Are the reasons you were given for your termination valid?

It could be that your employer has a bad reputation for treatment of injured workers. It could be that it has issued memoranda in which your injured worker status had been mentioned. That status may have been referred to in management or safety committee meetings. It could be that management has even gone out of its way to cause your co-workers to turn away from you and resent you because your filing spoiled their opportunity to receive their safety bonus.

Hopefully, this gives you a good idea of the specific evidence a lawyer looks for in that type of case. It is not expected that favorable evidence would exist with respect to all of the points of inquiry. That never happens. The matter comes down to whether, considering all of the evidence, pro and con, a jury would think it was more likely than not the employee was terminated because of the work related injury or claim filing. In a case of a termination allegedly because of some other protected activity or protected class status, this same approach is taken to evaluate it.

Evaluating the Problem of Your Case

There is no such thing as a perfect case. Do not be afraid to see a lawyer because of your perception that your case is not perfect. A lawyer may be able to win your case even though you were not the best worker or even though you may have done something to prejudice the case.

It is not uncommon for employees to have done something to make their case more difficult to win. You may have done something to prejudice your case, such as:

+ make prior inconsistent statements about your knowledge or lack of knowledge about the reason for the termination;

+ make prior admissions about your own average quality of work; or,

+ engage in *self-help*, such as telling the boss off.

However, it is not uncommon for employees not to know why they were terminated. Your lawyer, after carefully questioning you, is the one to try to figure that out. If you have told others that you do not know why the termination occurred, that is okay. Other evidence can establish the real reason for termination. Even when a jury hears that at one time the employee candidly admitted he or she did not know why the termination occurred, it may conclude—based on other evidence—that the termination occurred for the reason alleged in the employee's court complaint.

Further, if you admit your work contained some errors, that is not fatal. A jury knows that no one's work is perfect. It knows that an employer can criticize something about any worker if the employer looks hard enough. A plaintiff who admits that although he or she was a good worker, perhaps they were not the best worker, or that they made mistakes, has not necessarily harmed his or her case.

If you told the boss in crude terms what you thought of the termination or cursed at your boss—that hurts your case. It tends to rob it of its natural sympathy and weakens the identity between you and the jury. But if the evidence is that your boss provoked you into an outburst and that this behavior was out of character for you, it can serve to demonstrate the severity of the hostile work environment that was created by your boss.

In the face of claims by defense counsel that the plaintiff was not a good worker, many times it can be proven that the plaintiff was given good performance reviews and never heard any complaints about his or her work while employed. Even if there are some *complaints* about your work, it is not fatal to your case, because:

+ occasional complaints are expected;

+ what are characterized today as *complaints* were considered *suggestions* or *training* during employment;

+ others received the same complaints but were not terminated; and,

+ you received complaints when others did not for the same problems.

Evaluating Your Case when the Employer Covers Its Tracks

Employers, having become more wary of employment lawsuits, will often try to hide a wrongful discharge in a layoff due to a reorganization, reduction in force, or job elimination. In a lawsuit, however, the jury is allowed to look beneath the surface of a personnel action and scrutinize:

+ the circumstances that prompted the decision to combine or eliminate your position in the first place;

+ the process that determined who would be laid-off and on what basis;

+ whether the decision was subjective and, if so, whether the person who made the decision did so fairly and in accordance with the criteria the employer told him or her to follow; and,

✦ whether the reorganization achieved the employer's stated goal, so as to appear legitimate (rather than a cover for an unlawful discharge).

If your employer claims the layoff decision was prompted by legitimate business considerations that had nothing to do with you, it would be logical that business records, including management meeting minutes or notes, would bear that out. If economic necessity is blamed for the need to reorganize, financial reports and analyses would be expected to exist that disclose management thinking as to the headcount reduction number that would be required to achieve the desired economic benefit. During discovery, your lawyer can ask your boss in his or her deposition if such documents exist, and request that they be produced. Many times it turns out that the need for the layoff is not well-documented, and that lack of planning makes it easier to prove you were arbitrarily targeted. The strength of that evidence becomes particularly compelling when it turns out you were the only one in your department, or job group, to be let go.

Similarly, one would expect that if a legitimate layoff is undertaken, the employer will choose to retain its best people. Inquiry can be made during litigation as to the methodology employed by the employer to evaluate the merits of its own people. Bias is often allowed to come into play, either through the selection of spurious criteria for that evaluation or by allowing persons who would be motivated to retaliate to rate performance based on highly subjective factors.

Often, rating or ranking sheets exist that allow your lawyer to reconstruct the evaluation process and to enable them to ask the terminating manager about how they arrived at their numerical scores or grades. That examination may disclose ignorance or unwarranted assumptions by the firing manager about your comparator's supposed superior qualifications. It may also disclose that the terminating manager did not follow your employer's guidelines as to how candidates for layoff were to be evaluated. Seniority, for example, may have been rated on length of service in the department, rather than your employer's directive that it be rated on length of service with your employer.

Finally, even where documents exist that discuss and recommend a layoff or reorganization in months past, close examination may reveal that the layoff or reorganization that occurred is not the same one that was planned or recommended. It may be that those documents address a need to achieve a particular dollar reduction in labor costs and the actual layoff plan comes nowhere near achieving that objective. It may be that the documents speak to the need to reduce full-time positions in a different job category from yours, but you were targeted anyway. Evidence that the layoff that was effected was not the one that was planned helps demonstrate that it was not bona fide.

When a supervisor is notorious for his or her abusive treatment of employees, another favorite ploy of defense counsel is to argue that you have no case because your supervisor treated everyone like that. However, an unfair person rarely doles out unfair treatment fairly. Usually, there is something distinctive about the mistreatment you and other members of your protected class received at the hands of that supervisor.

If an employer denies the obvious and contends an unfair supervisor is a good supervisor, that strategy can backfire as well. If it instructs its management witnesses to protect that supervisor and downplay the horrors the supervisor has committed, that sets up a disparity between the testimony of the management witnesses and the testimony of the nonmanagement witnesses. That compounds the offense, for the jury views the employer not only as one which would engage in such conduct, but as one which would coerce others to perjure themselves to defend it.

Factors Affecting Your Case

A lawsuit is dynamic. Your lawyer will try to exploit any opportunities that your employer presents during litigation.

During the case, it may become apparent that:

+ a conspiracy existed to get rid of you;
+ your employer's witnesses were coached to modify the truth about your work performance;
+ your employer's witnesses gave inconsistent deposition testimony;
+ important documents were withheld or destroyed by your employer after the suit was filed;
+ your employer made threats to employees not to give favorable testimony about you; or,
+ your employer's witnesses lie on the stand.

Any of these factors will make a jury angry. Their presence erodes the employer's credibility on other matters and subverts its defense.

An employer may make other tactical errors to give you an advantage, such as by:

+ depreciating you;
+ underestimating your attorney;
+ taking an absurd position (*e.g.*, "No, it did not bother me when the plaintiff told the president he thought I was doing something illegal"); or,
+ blindly supporting your supervisor without having a reasonable basis for that support.

These mistakes are often committed. They are born out of arrogance. If an attitude of arrogance by the employer pervades the lawsuit, that may cause its failure in the case.

Other Factors that Can Help

Human nature and the nature of organizations have not changed much over the years. People tend to act to protect themselves—financially and emotionally. They act out of anger, fear, hatred, and vengeance. Companies tend to act to protect the continuity and vitality of the organization. These tendencies are powerful and consistent. As a result, your attorney may be aided during the case, because:

+ a wrongdoer seldom admits wrongdoing;

+ other people tend to allow wrongdoers to continue the wrongful acts;

+ management tends to support its managers, and therefore tends to discount the legitimate complaints as coming from workers who are disgruntled;

+ line managers often treat human resource managers as mere staff support;

+ sometimes human resource managers tend to be preoccupied with maintaining their own fragile relationship with the organization, resulting in a *shoot the messenger* stance; and,

+ many times, defense lawyers may tend to place a higher priority on retaining the employer as a client rather than being willing to tell the employer it did something wrong.

Your attorney may be further aided, because usually the wrongdoer is not forthcoming about the facts under questioning by the employer, and may provide outright denials or untruthful shadings of the truth. Your employer's human resource manager may not be able to get the truth from your employer's own people.

Similarly, persons in the workplace—by inertia—tend to allow wrongdoing to continue. For example, it is not infrequent that a general manager is allowed to sexually harass many women over a long period of time, even when other managers knew about it and knew it was part of their job to maintain a work atmosphere free of sexual harassment. It is far easier to ignore wrongdoing than to do something about it, particularly when the wrongdoer is your boss. As a result, the human resource manager cannot get the truth from subordinate witnesses, who take an *I did not see anything* approach.

Many human resource managers have a blind spot, too. Their job is to protect the employer. Some of them are more aggressive than others in recognizing potential liability, reporting it to their supervisors, and fixing a situation. Often, however, human resource managers are given responsibilities that involve inherent conflicts. On one hand, they are to clean up the system. So they report they have cleaned it up. On the other hand, they must report to upper management on new problems that may reflect poorly on their past performance in having cleaned up the system. This suggests to upper management that they may not have cleaned it up after all. As a result, human resource managers tend to want to put a *good face* on a problem. That may cause them to deny the problem that they supposedly fixed is continuing. This does not happen in every case, but it is a natural tendency.

Those same natural tendencies may extend to the investigation conducted by the employer's lawyer. All too often, the defense lawyer's first priority is to keep the client. The defense lawyer is not always in the best position to severely question or criticize their client's employees, particularly if the target of the plaintiff's case is the president who hired them. The result is a *they say* type of investigation, in which the lawyer accepts self-serving denials at face value. This response is not useful in resolving the case, or even in effectively promoting the employer's interests.

Therefore, despite what you perceive to be a disparity of power, because of the facts of your case, the dynamics of litigation, and the natural tendencies that cause employers to behave the way they do, you may have a real chance to win in court.

Chapter 15

Mistakes Employers Make

An employer who trains its managers tends to reduce its potential liability. Nevertheless, the same mistakes that lead to liability seem to be consistently repeated. It seems that no matter how much money an employer invests, so long as people continue to make employment decisions, liability will be generated. This chapter identifies the top ten mistakes employers make that lead to liability for wrongful discharge.

I told them about the harassment, but they did nothing about it.

An organization that refuses to listen to its employees, or is ill-equipped to do so, sets up a work environment that encourages rogue managers to run amok. Once unlawful harassment is reported, management must take effective, immediate, and corrective action designed to end the harassment. When they do not, wrongful discharge liability will follow.

After I told them about the harassment, they would not let it drop.

Conversely, some organizations overreact to complaints about harassment. Although the employee who has dared to make the complaint only wants to retreat, continue working, and be left alone, sometimes the overreactive employer simply will not let that happen. Instead, it becomes neurotic that a complaint has been made and refuses to let the employee retreat. Then, instead of focusing on the substance of the complaint, it all too often focuses on the complainant. The complainant is called into meeting after meeting to tell his or her story again and again. Eventually, the employee becomes frustrated and angry, and the employer, fearing the worst, begins to view the employee's story with scepticism and picks it apart. The employee finds that he or she is being cross-examined by amateur sleuths probing for weaknesses.

If action is taken on the complaint, the employer sometimes calls the employee back in to check to see if the employee is satisfied. In this process, the employer may *blame* the employee for making such a *big deal* of it or may start to inquire whether the employee is going to let things drop. Often, the last thing on the employee's mind is going to see a lawyer, until the employer suggests it.

Sometimes the employee is criticized about the manner in which the complaint was raised. Any number of things could serve as the basis for this employer mistake, including saying things such as:

- ✦ he or she could have spoken up sooner;
- ✦ he or she was too quick to complain;
- ✦ he or she failed to identify the culprit; or,
- ✦ he or she left out an important detail.

Workers do not want to get people in trouble. They just want to be left alone to work. Often, these post-complaint critique sessions themselves become a greater source of conflict than the initial reason for complaint.

They would not tell me what I did wrong.

Unless the employer gives you enough information about what you supposedly did wrong, there is no way you can defend yourself. Sometimes employers, in the interest of maintaining confidentiality, try to protect the identity of complainants. That is all right as far as it goes, but sometimes it is not only unreasonable, it is unrealistic to think the matter may be handled confidentially. The target of any investigation must be given sufficient information to be able to understand the charges they are to address.

They refused to follow up on the information I gave them.

In some cases, the employer receives and acts on a complaint but does not follow up on leads it receives to competently complete the investigation. This usually occurs when the employer wishes the investigation to lead to a particular result. This deprives the investigator of any interest in seeing to it that all leads are tracked.

They terminated me without hearing my side of the story.

It is good personnel practice in investigating charges of employee misconduct to withhold judgment until the investigation is complete. Before completing any investigation, it is good personnel practice to get both sides to the story. Sometimes, however, employees are terminated without being able to tell their side of the story. That only reinforces the notion that the employer was more interested in using the complaint as an excuse for termination, rather than in determining whether the complaint had merit.

All my supervisor did was criticize me.

When an employment relationship begins to disintegrate, it is easy to focus on the weaknesses of an employee's performance. All of us have weaknesses. If the employer wants to focus on those weaknesses exclusively, it can.

When someone is on the way out, though, it is easy to see whenever management has withdrawn its support. That period is characterized by relentless criticism. Almost anything that is accomplished is criticized. By this treatment, the employer sends the message that the employee is no longer welcome. It becomes clear the employer is invested in driving the employee from the workplace.

My supervisor was never clear about what was expected.

It is easy to tell someone what he or she is doing is wrong. It is much more difficult to tell them how to do it right. That takes active coaching. That takes time and energy. That usually requires establishing goals and objectives, and standards for measuring whether those goals and objectives have been attained.

Whenever it becomes apparent that a supervisor refuses to give you goals and objectives, it tends to show they are not interested in seeing you succeed. It suggests he or she has a different agenda.

They were setting me up for termination.

Employees know when the *fix* is in. The employer construes things the wrong way. The employee is given ambiguous instructions, or no instructions at all, and is then criticized for doing it the *wrong way*.

Employees can also tell the difference between the degree of support they are receiving versus their co-workers. They can also compare the relative training, coaching, or instruction they receive versus that of their co-workers. They know how much time their boss has spent with their office neighbor showing them how to do things. They also have keenly observed how their boss has reacted to any foul-ups their office neighbor has committed.

Frequently, the *set up* involves the establishment of unrealistic performance goals. A jury will look long and hard at whether the goals set for an employee are realistic and attainable, and whether any changes in those goals were justified.

They terminated me without following their own procedures.

Employees know if their employer tells its managers to utilize progressive discipline. Employees also know whether in past practice that has been the case. One of the easiest things for an employee to discern is whether they are being treated differently in that regard.

If your employer fails to follow its typical personnel practices in dealing with you, it may establish that you were subjected to differential treatment. That failure may serve as critical favorable evidence in your wrongful discharge case.

They terminated me just after I received a good performance review.

All too frequently the terminated employee will be able to pull out a recent favorable performance review that undercuts the strength of the employer's assertion that he or she was a poor performer. When that occurs, it suggests that during the interim period, his or her protected activity was to account for the change in attitude towards his or her work. Performance reviews are to be taken seriously by employers. A jury will hold them to whatever they say in those reviews.

Top Ten Complaints

1. *I told them about the harassment, but they did nothing about it.*
2. *After I told them about the harassment, they would not let it drop.*
3. *They would not tell me what I did wrong.*
4. *They refused to follow up on the information I gave them.*
5. *They terminated me without hearing my side of the story.*
6. *All my supervisor did was criticize me.*
7. *My supervisor was never clear about what they wanted.*
8. *They were setting me up for termination.*
9. *They terminated me without going through any of their own procedures.*
10. *They terminated me just after I received a good performance review.*

Chapter 16

Deciding Whether to Pursue Your Case

Once you accept an opinion that you have a case from an attorney with a respected reputation in the employment field, you must still decide whether to file it. Just because you have a case does not mean you should file it. You have other interests at stake. You should consider those other nonlegal factors in deciding whether to proceed. Those factors include:

+ your need for litigation;
+ the support of your family for this litigation;
+ your physical and emotional ability to undergo litigation; and,
+ whether this litigation will hurt more than help.

Your Need for Litigation

No case should ever be brought unless it needs to be, regardless of its merits. That need in an employment case is generally economic, but occasionally it is noneconomic as well. Only you can measure that need. But unless you have a need to pursue the case, you will soon find it tiresome, intrusive, and disruptive. You will end up fighting with your own lawyer for making demands on your time.

If you plan to move your residence during the course of litigation, that sense of disruption will only magnify. Long distance litigation is especially difficult and frustrating. You would need to incur travel expenses to have your deposition taken and to attend trial.

Plus, for weeks on end, it will seem that nothing is happening in your case. Litigation is slow, and it can be a source of aggravation if you let it. While an overriding need for litigation does not erase these irritants, its presence makes them easier to tolerate.

There are other frustrations. There may be interim expenses you may be billed for during litigation for court or litigation costs and lawyer's fees. Your spouse may grow tired of your preoccupation with the suit. You may grow more distant from your children during the case. All of these considerations indicate the the importance of using litigation as a last resort.

Your Support from Others for Litigation

Your ability to tolerate litigation will depend upon the level of support you have from your family. If your spouse was set against it initially, do not count on him or her changing his or her attitude towards it—ever—regardless of the outcome. That negative attitude can lead to fights, and in turn, to serious domestic instability, if not divorce. On the other hand, if your spouse is neutral or supportive, at least you would not have to concern yourself that domestic issues would be an additional stress factor that would make litigation even more unbearable.

Your Health

Your health is not an insignificant consideration in whether to go forward with a lawsuit. More than one case has been dismissed because the person suing experienced elevated blood pressure or had to seek counseling because of the stress associated with litigation. A good lawyer intends to spare you much of that stress through competent service that seeks to inspire confidence. You should expect them to responsibly reassure you about the status of your case through an honest and professional relationship, characterized by a free flow of information to you on an as-needed basis. However, no matter how competent and reassuring your lawyer, your angst may be implacable. The resulting stress may be too much for your physical and emotional health.

The Effect on Your Marketability

Finally, apart from the amount of money you may gain from the lawsuit, you will need to consider whether the filing of that lawsuit would impair your marketability at the very time you need to find a job. While the pursuit of an employment case is much more common than it was twenty years ago, and is more typically viewed as an aspect of the winding up of a business relationship, filing a lawsuit can still be harmful to your marketability with certain audiences. Some prospective employers may take the attitude they do not want to be next on your list. If you have already obtained subsequent employment, or plan to become self-employed, that would be less of a factor. Regardless, an immediate financial need to pursue a claim may not allow you to wait until you are reemployed.

If you are concerned that other employers in the industry would be put off by publicity associated with the filing of a multi-million dollar lawsuit, you have other options. One option would be to reduce your initial level of litigation visibility by first pursuing prefiling settlement efforts through demand letters, or, if necessary, the filing of an administrative complaint. Those measures seldom generate publicity. You could initiate litigation later after you become reemployed if your prefiling efforts are unsuccessful. On the other hand, if you are concerned that your former employer could hinder your efforts of finding another job, it may be best to hold off altogether until you have that next job. Once you make known to your former employer that you are contemplating legal action through a lawyer, if settlement negotiations fail at that stage, your former employer could tell prospective employers that you have threatened suit against them.

However, if the pretext for termination was a trumped-up charge of dishonesty, for example, it would do you no good to wait to press your legal rights while you pursue employment. The harm associated with the disclosure of the reason for termination in applications and interviews with prospective employers would do its own damage. Thus, sometimes litigation is necessary because you cannot afford to let the termination charges stand unchallenged.

Only after considering all of these nonlegal factors will you be in position to make a final decision whether to proceed.

Chapter 17

What to Expect During Litigation

Part of the anxiety associated with the decision of whether to file a lawsuit arises from one's unfamiliarity with the legal process. There is no real mystery to it. The legal system is highly formalized. The stages of litigation are distinct and predictable.

Prefiling Stage

After you retain a lawyer, but before your lawsuit is filed, you may be asked to assemble documents, provide a narrative, or arrange to have witnesses interviewed. Your lawyer is under a legal obligation to engage in *due diligence* to investigate your claim to the extent that is practicable before it is filed to avoid filing a frivolous lawsuit.

Demand Letters

Your lawyer may recommend sending a *demand letter* to the employer before your court case is filed to give the employer an opportunity to settle beforehand. A demand letter simply notifies the employer or its legal representative of your lawyer's representation, the reason for that representation, the facts that support your case, and the legal significance of those facts. It states that unless a settlement is reached, you will proceed with your case. If appropriate, it will contain an opening settlement demand. Sending a demand letter is particularly effective when the case is clearly documented or when it is thought the employer would attach value to avoiding the adverse publicity that sometimes attends a court filing. Generally, however, employees overestimate their employer's fear of lawsuits.

Only a relatively small percentage of cases are resolved with a prefiling demand letter. One reason is because employers know that many more lawsuits are threatened against them than are filed. Until a filing is made, the employer does not know for certain if a threat is real. As a result, employers and their lawyers are predisposed to say "No" in response to such letters. They believe they save money that way because a substantial number of cases do not survive that first round of opposition. Therefore, it takes exceptional circumstances for a case to stand out to the employer and merit settlement before filing. The employer must be convinced that simply saying "No" as usual will not be the end of the matter. That is also why it is important to attach yourself to a lawyer whose reputation is not to make idle threats.

ADMINISTRATIVE AGENCY COMPLAINTS

Sometimes the law requires that before you file a case in court, you must first *exhaust administrative remedies*. This is often the case if your wrongful termination implicates a federal or state discrimination statute. This administrative exhaustion requirement is satisfied by filing an administrative complaint of discrimination with a civil rights enforcement agency. For a list of such agencies in your area, see Appendix D. The agency will send you forms to complete if it believes it has jurisdiction over your case. Intake officers will gladly help you complete and file the forms properly. Once your administrative complaint is filed, your case will be assigned to an investigator, who may interview you and spend many weeks interviewing witnesses and requesting and reviewing documents.

This investigation is free and is sometimes very helpful. Indeed, without it your lawyer may not be willing to proceed. If your employer contends your performance was the reason for your termination, your lawyer may need the comfort level such an investigation brings before committing to litigation. If the stated reason was *attendance*, for example, and you do not possess your complete attendance records or a complete memory of your absenteeism, the administrative agency investigation will be the vehicle for your lawyer to learn the details of your attendance. Those investigations can take months to complete because of the backlog of other cases.

Cooperate with the investigator in any way that is requested. If the investigator needs additional information, provide it gladly and in a timely manner. While his or her work may take months to complete, feel free to check with the investigator periodically to see how the investigation is progressing.

The investigator will ask your former employer to respond to your complaint. The investigator will share the substance of that response with you and give you a chance to rebut any negative information you have heard.

At some point, the investigator will reach a decision about your case. It will then issue a written determination that either declares there is substantial evidence to support your case or states the evidence is insufficient. If the determination is in your favor, the agency will attempt conciliation (settlement) between the parties. If conciliation fails or is rejected, the agency will issue a *right to sue* letter, advising you that you have ninety days to pursue your claim in court. Even if the determination goes against you, you will receive the right to sue letter.

In some states, the EEOC has an agreement that the state will investigate the federal complaint on its behalf, along with a state charge. In those cases, once a determination is reached by the state, the case is sent to the EEOC to see if the federal agency agrees with the state determination. If the state determination was unfavorable to you, you will be given a chance to object to the determination and to ask the federal agency not to adopt it.

Once you receive the right to sue letter, your claim must be filed in court within the stated time period or else it will be barred by the statute of limitations. In the meantime, you have to go about the business of living your life, and let the legal process run on a separate track.

INTERVENING EVENTS

While your lawyer is waiting for a response to a demand letter and you both are waiting for the administrative agency to complete its investigation, events may transpire in your life that dictate the extent of your future involvement with the legal system. If, for example, you become reemployed at, near, or above the pay you were formerly making, the need for litigation can suddenly disappear. For some, the stress of litigation is as onerous as the stress the employer inflicted directly. Therefore, once you have obtained substitute employment, you may change the value you place on the pursuit of the case.

This is particularly true if your new work takes you to a different locale. It is difficult to maintain an appetite for long-distance litigation. To receive calls from a lawyer about the loss of a former job in a distant city quickly becomes an intrusion. If this happens to you, there is no shame in abandoning litigation that is no longer purposeful.

Trial Stage

A lawsuit is initiated through the filing of a formal court pleading known as the *complaint*. The complaint contains the various *claims* you are asserting. Those claims are stated through allegations of ultimate fact that are the basis for your case.

Once the complaint is filed it must be *served* with a *summons* on the party you are suing, the *defendant*. A *sheriff* or *process server* will effect service either by personal or another form of service permitted by law. Once the summons and complaint have been served, the defendant will have a certain amount of time, typically twenty or thirty days, to file a court *appearance*. During this time, the defendant will be turning the matter over to a lawyer, who will contact yours and give your lawyer notice of representation.

The opposing lawyer may ask your lawyer for an extension of time to investigate the matter before an appearance is filed. Extensions are routinely granted between lawyers out of professional courtesy. Do not worry. Such extensions typically will not cause undue delay. Besides, your lawyer may, and probably will, need to ask for an extension as well at some point in your case. Trust your lawyer's instinct as to when it is time to press the defendant for an appearance. Remember, if your lawyer is employed on a contingent fee basis, he or she will be just as motivated as you to resolve your case favorably and quickly.

DISCOVERY

After the case is filed, the parties will exchange what are known as *discovery requests*. Requests for production require each party to produce documents that may lead to relevant evidence. In addition, the federal courts and some states allow the service of *interrogatories*, that require the parties to answer questions in writing, under oath concerning relevant issues in the case. Once responses to the initial discovery requests have been given, the parties are ready to take depositions.

Depositions

A *deposition* is live testimony taken under oath in a question and answer format. Both sides take depositions. The opposing lawyer will take your deposition to find out about your case. The lawyer will ask you questions, and those questions and your answers will be stenographically recorded by a court reporter. Your lawyer will be there with you, ready to object to any improper questions, if need be. Your lawyer will prepare you for the deposition beforehand, so you will know what to expect. During your deposition, the opposing lawyer will ask all about your background, education, and work history. The lawyer will ask about your work for your former employer, the facts you have to support your lawsuit allegations, and your claimed damages. Your attorney will take the depositions of those responsible for your termination, any persons they relied upon for support or advice, and any other material witnesses who need to be deposed.

Next to the trial itself, the deposition stage is the most demanding of your time and energy during litigation. While your deposition may only last a day, or a part of a day, your lawyer will strongly encourage you to attend the depositions of the employer's witnesses. You will enjoy attending those depositions as well. It will be satisfying to see your boss finally have to account for his or her actions. Those depositions will vary in number and length, depending on the type of case and the number of actors involved. Currently, the Federal Rules of Civil Procedure forbid each side from taking more than ten depositions without asking the court.

MOTION FOR SUMMARY JUDGMENT

After the depositions are concluded and all documents have been exchanged, discovery is complete. At this juncture, the defendant may try to have your case dismissed by filing what is called a *Motion for Summary Judgment*. That motion contends the employee's case is so weak that, even after viewing all facts in favor of the employee, it is undeserving of submission to a jury and should be dismissed by the judge as a matter of law.

At summary judgment, a judge is not to resolve disputed issues of fact. To withstand such a motion, your lawyer's job is to show there is a genuine issue of material fact for a jury to resolve. For example, if the basis for the motion is your supposed poor performance in some area, your attorney would develop evidence that other employees who performed at that level were not terminated. About a quarter of all civil cases are disposed of on summary judgment. It is a nice hurdle to get past. Once you do, your case is scheduled for trial.

THE TRIAL

If your case is one of the few that are not settled earlier or disposed of at summary judgment, it will be tried. While the thought of a trial may cause you some anxiety, to go through a trial is not all that frightening. Indeed, a jury trial can be a very positive experience. There is nothing more satisfying than to be vindicated by a jury verdict. To go through a jury trial as a litigant can be difficult, but it is not nearly as arduous as one might imagine. In truth, a deposition can be more hostile, because there is no judge present at a deposition to supervise the deposing attorney. The demeanor of the opposing attorney is not tempered as it is at trial by the presence of a jury. At trial, lawyers are on their best behavior, so as not to raise a jury's ire or the wrath of a judge.

There are also not many surprises at trial. With modern rules of discovery, by the time of trial, both attorneys know who the witnesses are and what they will say. At trial, the lawyer's role is primarily to construct a persuasive and interesting, if not dramatic, presentation for the jurors.

Most of the stress you will experience during trial will not be externally imposed. It will be natural for you to worry, but your lawyer will help reduce your anxiety by preparing you in advance of your testimony and by communicating with you to let you know what is coming next at trial.

Most wrongful discharge cases can be tried in a week or so. Your attendance throughout the trial is essential. For most people, that can be arranged without adverse repercussions to their work or family life. Except for your daily attendance and preparation of your testimony, your role will be fairly inactive. Your attorney, though, will be frantically working twelve to fourteen hours a day analyzing the day's developments and preparing for the stages to follow. Be prepared to simply be on standby, ready to assist in providing information, or whatever other service your attorney requires. The trial experience will draw you and your lawyer together. Your interests will be furthered if you become a true partner with your lawyer in that effort.

The trial begins with jury selection, either by the attorneys or the judge, depending upon the jurisdiction. Then, each lawyer gives an opening statement. The purpose of the opening statement is to outline for the jury (without argument) the evidence each lawyer expects to present during the case. Next, the plaintiff's attorney presents the employee's case in chief through testimony and documentary evidence. After the plaintiff rests, the defendant proceeds with its case. At the close of the defendant's case, the plaintiff has the opportunity to present any rebuttal testimony.

Then, typically, the attorneys make their closing arguments to the jury. The judge then reads instructions to the jury to help them understand the controlling legal principles in the case. In some courts, the judge reads the instructions to the jury before the closing arguments. After that, the jury retires to deliberate and then renders its verdict.

POSTTRIAL MOTIONS

Even after the jury's verdict is rendered, the trial stage is not complete until after the filing and disposition of posttrial motions—a *Motion for New Trial* or a *Motion for Judgment Notwithstanding the Verdict*. Their purpose is to allow the trial judge to correct any injustice due to errors committed at trial. Their disposition requires weeks, if not months, of briefing and argument. Once the trial judge decides whether to take away the jury verdict (courts can do that) or order a new trial, the parties are given a period of time—typically thirty days—to appeal.

Appeal Stage

One reason people decide to settle is to avoid delay associated with the appeal that frequently follows a successful trial. In most court systems, a party is entitled to one appeal, so long as there is a legal basis for it.

The grounds for appeal vary. They usually relate to errors the judge made at trial, whether in rulings on the admissibility of evidence, instructions to the jury, or in failing to dismiss the case for insufficiency of the evidence. However, *reversible error* may be based upon a host of other factors, including misconduct of counsel, a witness, or even a juror.

An appeal can take a year or two (and sometimes more) to work through the appellate system. Appellate judges have no deadlines. While they work hard on their caseloads, their decisions are momentous. In our system, which is based on legal precedent, an appellate judge can decide a point of law that influences—if not determines—the outcome of similar cases that follow (perhaps forever). So appellate judges want to get it right.

Parties appeal by filing a simple document known as a *Notice of Appeal*. That begins the appellate process. A copy of the *Notice of Appeal* goes to a court reporter, who must then transcribe the entire trial. Once the lawyer who appealed obtains the court transcript, a briefing schedule is set. Then, after pouring over the transcript and doing whatever legal research is necessary, an opening brief is written by the lawyer who appealed. That usually takes a couple of months. Afterwards, the opposing lawyer is given time to file a responsive brief—typically thirty days. Following that, the lawyer who appealed is given another briefing period to file a reply brief. That concludes the briefing activity.

After all the briefs have been filed with the appellate court, the appellate judges (typically, there is a panel) will read and analyze them with the assistance of their law clerks. That process may take months. At some point, the appellate court may schedule oral argument. At oral argument, the court questions the attorneys about the points raised in their briefs. After oral argument, the appellate court issues its opinion *approving, modifying,* or *reversing* the lower court's judgment. Sometimes, that decision is rendered in weeks after oral argument. In other cases, the court's opinion may not be issued for many months. In the event the court overturns the decision, the case is usually *remanded* (sent back to the trial court) for a new trial. As you can imagine, it is not a process over which you or your lawyer have control. However, at any point along the road, settlement remains an option.

Irrespective of the foregoing explanation, no amount of information will entirely eliminate the stress you will inevitably feel prior to or during the litigation process.

Chapter 18

Things You Can Do to Help Your Lawyer Win

During much of the time that you are in litigation, you will feel helpless. You may be a hard-driving former CEO or a world-beater salesperson who is used to moving at top speed. All of a sudden, you are engaged in a pursuit where even though you are the main character, you are not in control. Still, in this strange new arena, there will be opportunities for you to assist your lawyer and further your own interests.

Provide Requested Information in a Timely Manner
The first homework you will probably be given by your lawyer is to draft a *narrative* of what occurred. A narrative is simply your story, in chronological order, of what occurred. No two narratives are alike. They can be six to sixty pages long. Whatever its length, it is important that you be complete and forthcoming in your narrative. It is equally important that you complete it and every other task your lawyer assigns to you in a timely manner.

During litigation, you will be asked to respond timely to discovery requests. Timing is everything in litigation. Poor impressions can be left with your opponent about your commitment to the case if discovery responses are not timely and forthcoming. If you delay inordinately in responding to discovery requests, your lawyer will have to start making excuses to request extensions. At some point, your lawyer will feel compelled to apologize to the other side for that delay. While a good lawyer always seeks to protect his or her client and take on the blame for any delay, eventually, the frustration with you may be too great for the lawyer to hide in conversations with the opposing lawyer. You really do not want your own lawyer having to make excuses for you. Nor do you want untimely responses to drive a wedge between you and your lawyer, or send a message of disinterest to your opponent. Be timely in your responses.

Stay in Communication with Your Lawyer

There will only be a handful of times your lawyer must be able to reach you immediately during your case. No one can predict when those occasions will arise. It is absolutely imperative that if you change your address or telephone number, you communicate any new directory information to your lawyer. Settlement windows come and go. Settlement offers are sometimes made on condition that they be accepted by the end of that same business day. With that condition imposed, such an offer would expire if not accepted within the given time. Do not let the delay associated with litigation delude you into a false sense that it is unimportant that you remain available to your lawyer at all times.

However, merely giving information to your lawyer about how to reach you is not enough. As a rule, if you get a call from your lawyer, he or she needs to talk to you right then. It may be that your lawyer needs to have you review a court paper for accuracy before it is filed or to have you provide information so he or she can complete it in a timely manner. Your lawyer may need to reach you to enable the scheduling of depositions or your trial. Therefore, return your lawyer's calls promptly. If you do not have voicemail, get it. If you do not have a cell phone, this would be a good time to buy one.

Treat Your Lawyer as a Member of Your Team

It is entirely appropriate for you to call your lawyer to ask what is going on or to express how you sincerely feel about what is going on. Your lawyer should be willing and able to give you an update, and even to address your anxieties. However, if you begin to exert artificial pressure on your lawyer to get things done on *your* schedule, you will create a negative impression of yourself with your own lawyer.

Most experienced trial lawyers are not shy about letting their clients know whenever they are *pushing too hard*. Some clients exert that pressure to obtain perspective about what is to be expected in this unfamiliar environment, and do so harmlessly. Other clients, if they are generally disagreeable, tend to display that trait during the rigors of litigation. If your former employer's stated reason for termination was that you lacked teamwork skills, it is best not to prove your employer's case in unpleasant exchanges with your own lawyer. You do not want to deprive your case of the wholehearted commitment by your lawyer it deserves, nor do you want to create doubt in your lawyer's mind about the merits of your case.

Be Flexible with Your Schedule

During the course of litigation, it may be that your deposition or trial has not been scheduled to your liking. While you are the central character, your schedule will—in most cases—be more flexible than that of the lawyers and judges who will be working on your case. If you demonstrate flexibility in scheduling, it will allow your lawyer maximum opportunity to timely complete the preparation of your case for trial.

Follow Your Lawyer's Advice

At various junctures during your case, you will receive advice from your lawyer about what to do and how to conduct yourself. While the practice of law is an art, not a science, assume that your lawyer knows what he or she is doing. If you are given advice, try to follow it.

The most common application of this principle relates to your performance during your deposition. Prior to your deposition, your lawyer will prepare you by giving you instructions that relate to your approach in responding to different types of deposition questions and techniques in answering questions. For example, you will be told not to volunteer information beyond the scope of the question. You may have had your deposition taken before. You may think you know what it is all about. However, listen to what your attorney on *this* case is telling you to do. While what you did in the past or what your former lawyer instructed you to do may not necessarily be inferior to the methodology your present lawyer advocates, if you have an attitude of superiority, you simply will not be perceptually set to listen to and take your lawyer's advice to heart.

Do Not Shoot the Messenger

At various stages of litigation, your lawyer will tell you how the case is going. Sometimes you will initiate the discussion. Sometimes your lawyer will. A common event that precipitates that discussion is your deposition and the depositions of the employer's witnesses. If, during those discussions, your lawyer gives you some bad news, including about your own performance, do not get mad at your lawyer. You want to have a lawyer who will be candid with you and deliver the truth to you about developments in the case, good or bad. If your lawyer criticizes you, do not take that as an act of betrayal. Instead, think of your lawyer as a boxing coach critiquing your performance in your corner of the ring between rounds. Just as a boxer needs that feedback, so do you.

Try to Control Your Relatives

The most difficult thing an experienced employment attorney has to cope with during the initial interview is the *helpful spouse*. Your lawyer needs to be able to quiz you and even to place you on the defensive during that initial interview without your spouse coming to your rescue. If you are placed on the witness stand, no one will be able to help you. One function your lawyer performs during the initial interview is to size you up as a witness. If you encourage your spouse to remain a spectator, you will be doing yourself and your lawyer a great service.

Likewise, during the course of litigation, and particularly during settlement discussions, it is important to understand that if you were the one terminated, your lawyer has an attorney-client relationship with you, not your spouse. Your lawyer is not at liberty during your case to share confidential information with your spouse without your consent. In the late stages of a case, it is a bit awkward after working with a client for the better part of a year for a lawyer to have to deal with the client's spouse in settlement discussions.

That is not to say that it is improper for your spouse to be involved in settlement discussions if need be. In some cases, a lawyer takes a chance not to include a domineering spouse in a mediation. However, throughout the litigation, what should be respected is that it is your case and no one else's. You are the one who was damaged by the termination. You are the primary party who has to live with the lawsuit and the consequences of settling or proceeding to trial.

Do Not Fall in Love with Your Case

Some clients, somewhere after they file their lawsuit, become lost in the fantasy that they will reap untold riches if a jury hears their case. They may indulge in that fantasy even though their lawyer had pointed out the problems in their case. Those problems may have been reflected in the probability of success their lawyer gave to them initially.

Some clients read about a multi-million dollar recovery in a different case and convince themselves that is what they will get. Maybe it is because of their own sense about how much they had gone through. Whatever the reason, a disconnect can develop between the lawyer and the client, based on their differing notions of the value of the case.

If such a disconnect occurs, it often requires a lot of work on the part of the lawyer to dissuade the client from his or her position. Sometimes the effort that is required can jeopardize the lawyer-client relationship. Sometimes it takes the help of a third party, such as a mediator, or even in rare cases, the client's spouse, to bring the client down to earth.

Do Not Pull Any Surprises

Good cases can take a turn for the worse. One way they can do that is if you say or do something that changes the status quo. Most clients do not realize it, but their posttermination actions can adversely affect the *winability* and value of their case. Actions with that potential take many forms. Some of those developments are totally within their control. Others may be unavoidable. The events that can have an effect on liability or damages in your case include:

- ✦ filing a bankruptcy action;
- ✦ termination by a subsequent employer;
- ✦ intervening criminal activity;

+ an acrimonious divorce;
+ inappropriate contact with your former employer;
+ inappropriate contact with witnesses;
+ ceasing to look for work;
+ going back to school; and,
+ engaging in misconduct or theatrics during trial.

The potential effect of those developments on the outcome of litigation need not be explained. Yet, all too often the lawyer is the last to know of their occurrence. Try not to pull any surprises. If something unexpected should occur, forget about the embarrassment and notify your lawyer immediately. This gives him or her the maximum opportunity to repair any damage.

Keep the Faith

A lawsuit is an ordeal. There will be the inevitable ups and downs as your case progresses. At trial, you will be on an emotional roller coaster from day to day. You may even lose the case at trial, only to see it revived on appeal. Rest assured that your lawyer will be sharing that same emotional ride. Through it all, you maximize your chances of ultimate victory by not succumbing to the temptation to blame others in the event of a defeat in battle. A good lawyer tries to turn every negative into a positive. They are duty-bound by the code of professional responsibility to zealously represent your interests. Most employment lawyers who are successful personally associate themselves with their client's cause. If you chose your lawyer wisely, do not lose faith in the face of a defeat. Remain steadfast in your commitment to see it through.

Ways to Help Your Lawyer Win

1. Provide requested information in a timely manner.

2. Stay in communication with your lawyer.

3. Treat your lawyer as a member of your team.

4. Be flexible with your schedule.

5. Follow your lawyer's advice.

6. Do not shoot the messenger.

7. Try to control your relatives.

8. Do not fall in love with your case.

9. Do not pull any surprises.

10. Keep the faith.

Chapter 19

Common Questions About Case Settlements

Most cases that are filed eventually settle. There is risk to litigation for both sides. In most cases, both parties ultimately conclude it is in their own best interest to try to come to terms to avoid the risk of losing.

The days when it was a sign of weakness to mention the settlement first are long gone. In fact, a skillful lawyer can punctuate a favorable development by behaving as if, in light of that development, the other side would surely want to discuss settling the case. While the process of settlement is no mystery to lawyers, you may have some questions about the process and what to expect.

Q: If I get a lawyer and file a case, does that mean the case will not settle?

No. Over 80% of civil cases are settled after they are filed. During the course of litigation, several *settlement windows* (opportunities) will appear. Those windows typically relate to anticipated or concluded events in the case. During each window of opportunity, which may last but a few days, the lawyers are temporarily on hold—having just finished one activity and about to commence another. Because cases cannot remain long in a static position, the settlement window closes when one of the attorneys chooses to put the case back in gear. Lawyers only know two speeds—*go* and *stop*. If your attorney is skillful, he or she will be sensitive to the opportunities that present themselves.

Settlement windows typically open at the following times:

+ on receipt of a prefiling demand letter;
+ just after the case is filed;
+ after depositions are taken;
+ after surviving a pretrial summary judgment motion to dismiss;
+ just before preparation for trial; and,
+ at or after trial.

Rarely do both parties believe it is in their interest to settle at the same time.

Q: *Can I save money by first trying to settle the case myself?*

Typically, no. This holds true for three reasons. First, without sound legal advice, you may engage in an unsound negotiating strategy. You may think you are only trying to simplify matters if you get right to your bottom line. The problem is that even if a party characterizes an offer as their bottom line, the tendency is for people not to believe that. It is highly unusual for a party to accept an initial offer. Once you put a value on your case, you may *box in* your lawyer and make it difficult for him or her to negotiate for more than the figure your former employer has already been advised to reject.

Second, you may not appreciate the full value of your case and set your settlement sights too low. There may be other aspects of settlement, such as the noneconomic factors associated with a guarantee of good job references, that you have not considered.

Third, if your case is substantial, no one will pay you a substantial settlement without an attorney. Your ability to attract a knowledgeable and experienced attorney demonstrates to your former employer that someone who has a track record in such matters is convinced your case has substantial value. Your former employer knows that if one person can be convinced of that, perhaps a jury can be as well. Having an attorney also tells your former employer that if it does not settle with you, it will be in it for the long haul. That represents not only significant cost, but also potential disruption to its business. It is seldom that an attorney cannot bring more value to your case than the fee that attorney will earn.

Q: What is my case worth in settlement?

There is no book to refer to in valuing an employment case. That is why it is important to seek out an experienced practitioner in the field who has a sense for the value of your case in your market area. Each case will have its own value, depending on a number of different factors. Those factors include:

- ✦ the type of damages recoverable for that type of case in your jurisdiction;
- ✦ the amount of money you have lost or stand to lose;
- ✦ the emotional distress or injury to reputation you have suffered;
- ✦ the egregiousness of the employer's conduct;
- ✦ your personal jury appeal;
- ✦ the jury appeal of your antagonist;
- ✦ the probability your case will survive a pretrial motion to dismiss;
- ✦ the probability of a favorable jury verdict; and,
- ✦ the size of your former employer.

Q: *If we try to settle now and are unsuccessful, can we ask for more at trial?*

Yes. Settlement discussions are confidential and will not be admissible at trial. The judge and jury will not hear any numbers that were discussed during settlement discussions.

Q: *What can I get in settlement besides money?*

If you do not settle, all a jury can do is give you money. In wrongful discharge cases in which a discrimination statute has been violated, the judge has injunctive power to order reinstatement. There may be other things that are just as important to you that only a settlement can provide.

Typically, noneconomic factors, such as favorable job references, an agreed-upon procedure for responding to employer inquiries, and an agreement not to disparage you, are all terms that can be negotiated. Anything the parties agree upon can be placed into a settlement document.

Q: *My lawyer has mentioned something about mediation? What is mediation?*

Mediation is a process whereby a third party attempts to work with the plaintiff and defendant to try to facilitate a settlement. Mediation is not *arbitration*. A mediator does not decide the case— an arbitrator does. Typically, the parties jointly select a third party to serve as mediator and a date is set for mediation.

Before mediation, each attorney submits materials for the mediator to read, so he or she can become familiar with the facts of the case and the legal issues that are involved. Many mediators also ask the attorneys to provide the negotiating history of the case, their candid assessment of the strengths and weaknesses of their case, what they think the other side will pay to settle it, and a range their client may ultimately deem acceptable. At mediation, the mediator does shuttle diplomacy, taking offers and counter-offers back and forth until the case is either settled or settlement fails.

From the employee's perspective, settlement is a no-lose proposition. If the amount offered in settlement at mediation is insufficient, the case proceeds as if mediation had never occurred.

Chapter 20

Special Rights and Benefits Legislation

Special legislation has been enacted by both Congress and the state legislatures that address the problems of terminated workers outside the traditional discrimination, retaliation, and whistle-blowing context. That legislation addresses the worker's need for continuing pay or benefits, and the integrity of their pension plans. The legislation also grants special protection to workers terminated for taking advantage of government-mandated benefits, including family leave. The principal federal legislation that protects those rights are discussed in this chapter.

Unemployment Compensation

An unemployment compensation program has been established in every state and the District of Columbia. Benefits are restricted to *employees*, but that term may include persons called *independent contractors* if the applicable requirements are satisfied. Labels are not determinative.

Each state has its own eligibility rules. In all states, people are eligible only if they earn a required minimum amount during the *base period*. The base period is defined in most states to include the first four calendar quarters of the last five full quarters before the claim filing. Most also require the employee to be employed for a minimum time during that period, typically at least two of the calendar quarters during the base period.

Unemployment compensation is designed to provide assistance only to those who are ready, willing, and able to work. Therefore, if a person is ill or disabled, and cannot engage in any work, they are not eligible. They also must be actively seeking work to remain eligible.

A person is disqualified from receipt of benefits in all fifty states and the District of Columbia if terminated for *misconduct*. That term is variously defined. It does not include mere *inadequate performance*. It typically requires evidence of *willful* behavior. Sometimes it is defined to also include repeated acts of negligence, despite repeated warnings. In some states, the disqualification is only for a period of weeks, unless the misconduct was particularly *gross*. In most states, the disqualification is for the duration of the period of unemployment. (For a state-by-state list of the length of disqualification from receipt of benefits for misconduct, see Appendix C.)

In all fifty states and the District of Columbia, a person who voluntarily resigns his or her position forfeits the right to benefits if the resignation was without *good cause*. In most states, an employee who resigns without good cause loses his or her benefits during the whole period of employment. In most states, the employee who resigns with good cause is still ineligible, unless the employee is able to prove the good cause was attributable to the employer or was connected to the work. In those states, a purely personal reason will not be deemed sufficient justification.

Health Insurance Legislation—Consolidated Omnibus Budget Reconciliation Act (COBRA)

COBRA requires certain employers to offer health plan continuation coverage to employees and their dependents who would otherwise lose their group coverage due to certain *qualifying events,* such as termination, divorce, or death of the employee. A termination for *gross misconduct* is disqualifying.

Not all employers are covered. Employers having fewer than twenty employees are exempt. However, for purposes of COBRA, independent contractors are included in the count.

Following a qualifying event, the employer is required to give notice to the eligible participant of his or her rights under COBRA. The employer must notify the plan administrator within thirty days of an employee's termination or other qualifying event. The plan administrator must notify the participant of the right to elect continuation coverage within fourteen days thereafter. The notice should contain adequate information about the coverage offered and its cost. The participant must notify the employer of the election to continue coverage within sixty days of receiving notice. The notice must be given in writing.

Thereafter, the participant must pay the insurance premium that is due. The insurance that is offered must have the same coverage that the participant had before the qualifying event.

Generally, COBRA eligibility lasts for eighteen months. Eligible persons who are disabled for Social Security purposes at the time of termination may continue COBRA coverage for a total of twenty-nine months, but at a premium rate for the additional months. There are some circumstances in which coverage can be extended to a total of thirty-six months for a spouse or child, but never for a terminated employee.

The Health Insurance Portability and Accountability Act (HIPPA)

HIPAA provides legal protection for employees and their dependents covered by a group health insurance plan. HIPAA limits exclusions for preexisting conditions and prohibits discrimination on the basis of an employee's health status. Under some circumstances, it allows special opportunities to enroll in a new plan. It also gives employees rights to purchase individual coverage if they have no group health coverage available and have exhausted their COBRA rights.

Retirement Legislation — ERISA

Section 510 of the *Employee Retirement Income Security Act* (ERISA) prohibits employers from interfering with the receipt of benefits covered by that Act. *ERISA* protection extends beyond mere interference with pension or retirement benefits. The Act also regulates employee *benefit plans* for active employees, including health insurance plans and other employee welfare plans to which a participant may become entitled. Thus, many cases have found violations of ERISA when an active employee used or was about to use a welfare benefit.

Under ERISA, while an employer may reserve the right to discontinue a welfare benefit plan, it may not otherwise discriminate against or discharge a worker for the purpose of interfering with his or her anticipated right to receive benefits.

Notice of Plant Closure Legislation

Employers having at least 100 employees must give their employees and unions sixty days' advance notice of a plant closing or mass layoff, pursuant to the *Worker Adjustment and Retraining Act* (WARN).

A *plant closing* means the permanent or temporary shutdown of a single site of employment, or one or more facilities or operating units within a single site of employment, if the shutdown results in the loss during any thirty-day period of fifty or more employees (excluding part-time employees).

Employee Leave Legislation

Since 1990, state and federal legislators have enacted pro-family legislation to allow persons who work for certain employers to remain at home after the birth or adoption of a child or for medical reasons. The rights are conferred only to persons who work for employers having over a certain number of employees. There are conditions to asserting these rights. The leave periods are of limited duration. The employer is not required to pay the employee who takes a leave—except existing benefit rights, such as vacation or sick leave, may be applied during the leave period.

Basic Provisions

On August 5, 1993 the *Family and Medical Leave Act* (FMLA) took effect. This legislation requires employers having fifty or more employees to allow leave to employees under certain circumstances. In states that have state leave laws, the employee is entitled to whichever benefit is greater under the two laws, although the leave period may run concurrently.

FMLA grants eligible employees up to twelve work weeks of leave during a twelve-month period for the following purposes:
+ to care for a child following its birth;
+ to care for a child placed with employee for adoption or foster care;
+ to care for a family member (spouse, parent, or child) of the employee when the family member has a serious health condition; or,

◆ when an employee has a serious health condition that makes the employee unable to perform the functions of his or her position.

An *eligible employee* under FMLA is an employee who has been employed for at least twelve months by the employer. The employee must have worked for at least 1,250 hours of service with the employer during the previous twelve-month period. The employee must also work at a worksite where the employer employs fifty or more employees within seventy-five miles. In contrast, state leave legislation may apply to smaller employers, or in favor of employees employed for a shorter period.

A *serious health condition* under FMLA is defined broadly. It includes illness, injury, impairment, or physical or mental condition that involves:

◆ inpatient care for any period;

◆ continuing treatment by a health-care provider for a period of incapacity; or,

◆ that is related to a chronic serious health condition.

Notice to the employer is required in accord with employer policy, not to exceed thirty days' notice in cases where the need for the leave was anticipated, and as soon as practical in other cases.

Upon conclusion of the leave, the employer is required to reinstate the employee to the position held at the time the leave was required or to an *equivalent position*. An equivalent position is one that has the same pay, benefits, working conditions, and similar duties and responsibilities.

Under FMLA, it is unlawful for an employer to interfere with or deny the exercise of the right to medical leave. It is also unlawful for an employer to discharge or otherwise discriminate against an employee for opposing an unlawful employment practice under FMLA.

FMLA and the ADA

Sometimes employers mistakenly believe FMLA supercedes (instead of works in conjunction with) the *Americans with Disabilities Act* (ADA). They mistakenly believe that if an employee exhausts his or her FMLA leave and is still unable to return to work, the employee may be terminated at that point. However, even after you take your twelve weeks of FMLA leave, if you are disabled, an additional leave of absence from work may be a *reasonable accommodation* under the ADA.

You should not be confused into thinking that a *serious health condition* under FMLA is necessarily a *disability* under the ADA. The two are not necessarily the same. Still, it is possible that if you meet the definition of a disabled person under the ADA, took FMLA leave, and were then terminated, you may bring claims under both statutes if they are supported by the facts of your case.

Chapter 21

12 Steps to Build Your Workplace Power

If you could look into a crystal ball and anticipate a termination by six months or more, you would be in better position to avoid its occurrence. If you could see it foretold, would that not compel you to put a plan of action into effect in an attempt to change your fate? If so, is it not a fair question to ask, "Why would you not be doing that all along?" After all, no one knows if or when he or she will be terminated. It is a risk everyone bears at all times. That being the case, everyone should be more proactive to prevent it.

There are twelve steps you can take to consolidate your workplace power. These steps are simple. In most cases they get down to basic workplace etiquette. However, it is surprising how frequently the considerations behind the steps are disregarded. This plan will only serve you well if you work with it. Think of other steps. Tailor your own plan to your work environment and to the personality of your supervisor.

Step One—
Learn to Like the People You Work With

It takes all kinds of people to make a company run. Some will be men, some women. Some will be educated, some not. Some will not be of your faith or philosophy. Some will not be of your color or national origin. Many will be from different regions of the country, with different social norms than you are used to.

You may not be an extrovert. But if you send off signals that you do not like the people you work with, they will know it—and they will not like you either. So the first thing to do is to find something about each person you can respect. Whenever you see that person, think of that aspect of their personage and give them a little smile. Pretty soon, you will find that they will take an interest in who it is exactly that would give them such positive feelings. In this world, a little personal interest goes a long way. Remember, if you like them, they will like you.

Step Two—
Communicate Often with Your Supervisor

The biggest frustration of many supervisors is that the people they are supervising just *do not get it*. To them, their subordinates may be able to perform tasks if requested, but they are missing the point of their mission. If, through casual conversation with your supervisor, you can communicate that you understand what you are there to do and are excited about where the department is going, you will be seen by your supervisor as one of the few who *do get it*.

Step Three—Never Turn Down an Invitation

Following steps one and two still does not make you one of *the guys*. There will be occasions in which you are asked to join the boss or the group for lunch or other social event. Never decline such an invitation. Otherwise, that may send a signal that you think yourself *too good* to be with them. Those who think their interests may be advanced by doing so may begin to take action to ostracize you from the group. If you work in a highly competitive environment, your refusal may play right into the hands of your chief rival.

Step Four— Do Not Be Afraid to Socialize with Your Boss

If your boss goes to lunch with other co-workers when asked, your boss will think it odd if you never extend an offer. If there is some question as to your supervisor's amenability to such an overture, take a chance. Even if your supervisor rejects the invitation, he or she will be pleased to be invited. That may lead to reciprocal invitations from your supervisor. Once you get to a lunch that you invited your supervisor to, you buy—even over an objection— unless you sense your boss would be offended by that gesture. The last thing you want is for your timidity to be misconstrued by your boss as a signal you would rather not socialize with them. Further, it is not prudent to allow your boss to be solely courted by your chief rival in the department.

Step Five—Socialize with Your Co-Workers

If your co-workers see you taking the boss out for lunch frequently, they will naturally tend to become jealous and label you a *brown noser*. Your attentions cannot be directed upwards only, or you will be accused of *managing up*. That will leave you open to being stabbed in the back. In fact, you must go out with your co-workers about three times more frequently than with your boss for your co-workers to trust you. On these occasions, if they know you have just lunched with the boss and you have some news you are free to share from your meeting with your boss, they may even come to view you as a useful and important ally.

Step Six—
Make Your Co-Workers Feel
Good about Themselves

No one can carry a department alone. It takes all the people in it working together for it to function as designed. Some people, however, do themselves a disservice by viewing themselves as the only *key employee* in the department. While any department has its key workers, everyone is supposed to contribute something of value. The truth is that unless the performance of each of the people around you furthers the interests of your employer, they would not be around.

Try to understand and appreciate the key contributions made to the group by each of your co-workers. If you can identify the value each contributes and compliment them on it, that will deflect any charge that you are a only interested in promoting yourself. Give the praise publicly. If you do it and mean it, you will have a friend for life.

Step Seven—
Do Not Forget Who Brought You to the Dance

You may have been recruited to the company by a particular officer or manager. You may never have worked for that person, or may have only done so for a little while until one of you was moved or promoted. It is imperative that you do not let that person, forget your never-ending thanks for being invited into the company. Keeping communication open through lunches and dinners and remembering special occasions such as birthdays will keep that person's door open to you in a time of crisis.

Step Eight—Never Violate a Confidence

When it comes to office politics, people need to know who they can trust. People talk in the workplace. Some value themselves based upon the *information* they can impart to others. If you follow the other steps in this plan, your co-workers will soon try to impress you with the information they impart to you. You need to keep sensitive information to yourself. Refrain from the temptation of passing that information on to others, even when you think that might do you some good. If you become known as one who would divulge confidential personal information given to you by others, you will never be kept *in the loop* again. Moreover, if the person to whom you divulge is a supervisor, you will be branded a turncoat and ostracized by your peers.

Step Nine— Never Refuse an Assignment if You Can Help It

You may have been hired to do one job. Since then, your department may have experienced layoffs and your boss may have asked others to pick up additional duties. In other cases, your boss may wish to cross-train department staff so the workforce as a whole can become more flexible. The thing to remember is that you do not own your job. If your boss can take it away because you are an employee at will, your boss can change it (at least in the private, nonunion sector).

If you are a union employee or a government worker, your job classification may have been bargained for or adopted by ordinance. Even so, management retains great discretion to assign work within a particular job classification. In still other cases, your boss may have identified you as a particularly talented candidate for promotion, but cannot put you up for promotion until you learn several positions, machines, or work stations. To the extent you are free of any union or classified service restraint, if you refuse a request to take on more work, especially in the aftermath of cutbacks when others are asked to do the same, you will automatically be viewed by your supervisor as a person of limited utility. That may make you expendable in the next round of layoffs.

Step Ten—Know Your Supervisor's Expectations

Some bosses are clearer than others in telling you what they want and when they want it. Some are habitually vague about it. Others are timid and do not want to be viewed as unreasonable ogres. Whatever the case, you are the one who is responsible for doing the work, and doing it *right* and *on time*. It is always a good idea when you are given an assignment—particularly verbally—to confirm what it is you are being asked to do and by what date.

Step Eleven—Never Speak Ill of the Company

No company is perfect. There is always something to complain about at work. Let others *bad-mouth* the company or your supervisor if they want. Do not put yourself in the position of having your negative comments parroted back to you by your boss or human resources. You do not need to excuse yourself from the company of your co-workers when they engage in that conduct, so long as the speaker is not so open and loud that your presence could be misconstrued to be public approval or support for the negative comments.

Step Twelve— If You Are Unhappy, Do Not Broadcast It at Work

You may come to the point when you will be actively seeking other work. If you let that be known, your employer will gladly give you the opportunity to make your job search a full-time proposition. No company wants to retain someone in its employ who is open about his or her desire to leave. If you are unhappy in your work, there will be a great temptation to let your unhappiness be known to others and to lead them to believe that you are actively looking for work elsewhere—even when you are not. If you value your next full paycheck, resist that temptation.

The 12 Steps

1. Learn to like the people you work with.
2. Communicate often with your supervisor.
3. Never turn down an invitation.
4. Do not be afraid to socialize with your boss.
5. Socialize with your co-workers.
6. Make your co-workers feel good about themselves.
7. Do not forget who brought you to the dance.
8. Never violate a confidence.
9. Never refuse an assignment if you can help it.
10. Know your supervisor's expectations.
11. Never speak ill of the company.
12. If you are unhappy, do not broadcast it at work.

Epilogue

Hopefully, this book provides you with guidance to help you through your current workplace crisis and makes all your employment experiences to come easier to deal with. No book can prevent difficulties from arising in a workplace setting. The dynamics of organizations and the interplay of relationships are so complex that occasional problems will inevitably arise. Perhaps the ideas and suggestions contained in this book will stimulate the development of your workplace skills so that future moments of crisis will pass harmlessly.

However, if nothing you can do prevents an infringement on your employment rights, I hope this book demystifies the legal system for you and aids you in your pursuit of full vindication.

Glossary

A

Americans with Disabilities Act (ADA). A federal statute concerning discrimination against persons with disabilities.

administrative remedy. A quasi-judicial proceeding before an administrative agency charged to enforce a law.

appeal. The stage of a lawsuit during which the disposition of a case at the trial level is reviewed for errors.

arbitrator. A person who decides issues in dispute in an arbitration proceeding.

arbitration. A nonjudicial proceeding used to decide cases as an alternative to trial, typically under more relaxed rules and procedures.

at-will employment. Employment that is terminable without cause.

B

backpay. Lost wages from the date of termination to the date of trial.

breach of contract. A violation of an enforceable promise.

C

civil law. Law that regulates the affairs of people and entities other than criminal law.

claim for relief. A legal theory advanced by a party in a civil court pleading.

Consolidated Omnibus Budget Reconciliation Act (COBRA). A federal statute that allows for the continuation of health insurance coverage after employment is terminated.

common law. Judge-made law based upon case precedent.

complainant. The charging party in an administrative proceeding.

complaint. The legal document that starts a lawsuit.

contract. A legally enforceable agreement.

D

damages. The monetary relief a person in a lawsuit is requesting to be awarded.

defamation. A verbal or written statement that injures a person's reputation.

defendant. The person or entity against whom a lawsuit is brought.

demand letter. A letter from an attorney to a party that sets forth the basis for a claim and demands the payment of money or some other remedy.

deposition. An interrogation under oath by an attorney after a lawsuit is filed.

discharge. An involuntary termination of employment.

disclaimer. A statement that purports to negate a promise.

discovery. The pretrial phase of a lawsuit, during which parties exchange information.

discrimination. To treat someone differently from the treatment given to others, which is unlawful only if the differential treatment is because of protected class status or activity, such as race, sex, age, etc.

disparate treatment. To treat members of a particular protected class differently from others.

due process. Procedural fairness, typically found in public or union employment, that requires notice of charges and a fair opportunity to be heard.

E

economic damages. Monetary relief a party seeks in a lawsuit equal to the economic loss the party has sustained, such as lost wages.

Equal Employment Opportunity Commission (EEOC). The federal administrative agency charged with investigating discrimination claims.

Employee Retirement Income Security Act (ERISA). A federal statute regarding the regulation of retirement accounts and certain other employment benefits.

F

Family and Medical Leave Act (FMLA). A federal statute that requires employers to provide unpaid leave to employees and certain family members under certain circumstances relating to childbirth, adoption, or a serious medical condition.

fraud. An intentional or reckless misrepresentation by commission or omission.

G

grievance. An internal remedy, typically given to union workers, to contest an adverse personnel action.

H

Health Insurance Portability and Accountability Act (HIPAA). A federal statute allowing for immediate and continued health care coverage for employees switching employers.

hostile work environment. A charge in a constructive discharge or discrimination case that the employer's adverse acts are so frequent or severe that hostility pervades the working environment.

I

independent contractor. A party who is hired by another, but is not under the control of the other with respect to the manner or means of doing the work, so that an employment relationship is not formed.

injunction. A court order that compels a party to do or refrain from doing something.

intent. A state of mind in which an actor purposefully acts intending to cause injury, or with knowledge that if the act occurs, it is substantially certain injury will result.

interrogatory. A written question that must be answered in writing under oath by a party in a civil lawsuit.

J

just cause. Having a good reason to act.

L

layoff. A termination of employment, typically because of a reduction in force.

liability. A legal obligation one party owes to another.

litigation. The legal activity associated with a civil lawsuit.

M

mediation. A dispute resolution process whereby a third party is used to facilitate a voluntary settlement between the parties.

mediator. A person who, unlike an arbitrator, does not decide which party prevails, but instead serves as a facilitator to help the parties voluntarily settle a lawsuit.

memorialize. To make a written record of some event.

N

noneconomic damages. Monetary relief a party seeks in a lawsuit other than for lost income and expenses, such as for emotional distress or injury to reputation.

O

Occupational Safety and Health Act (OSHA). A federal statute concerning workplace safety.

P

performance improvement plan. A tool used by management to correct substandard performance that sets ascertainable goals for a stated period.

plaintiff. The person or entity that initiates a lawsuit.

private sector employment. Employment other than with a government body.

probationary period. The initial period of employment that must be served before an employee acquires full rights, which may include the right not to be terminated except for just cause.

progressive discipline. A disciplinary system that involves ascending levels of discipline if performance does not improve after notice. This typically including a verbal warning, followed by at least one written warning before termination.

protected activity. Activity that is given legal protection from retaliation by statute or case decision because it furthers an important public policy.

protected class. A classification of persons to which Congress or a state legislature has afforded legal protection against discrimination or retaliation.

public sector employment. Employment with a government body.

punitive damages. Damages awarded not to compensate a victim for damages suffered, but to punish the defendant and set an example for others.

Q

qualified privilege. In the law of defamation, a conditional right to speak ill of another, which is lost if abused in certain ways.

R

reasonable accommodation. An adjustment or allowance that employers are required to give to disabled workers to enable them to perform their work, such as a job modification, a work aid, or a leave of absence.

recklessness. A state of mind in which a person acts without regard to the consequences that will likely result from their acts, or with an *I do not care* attitude.

reinstatement. As a remedy in a discrimination case, a court order that the employee be rehired.

remedy. The type of relief to which a prevailing party in a lawsuit is entitled.

respondent. The party against which an administrative complaint is brought.

retainer agreement. A document that formalizes an attorney-client relationship and expresses its terms.

right to sue letter. A letter issued by a federal or state administrative agency that grants to the party to whom it is issued the right to initiate a lawsuit within a stated period of time.

S

settlement. An agreed upon resolution of a lawsuit by the parties.

sexual harassment. Verbal or physical conduct of a sexual nature that is unwelcome and would be offensive to a reasonable victim.

statute. An act of Congress or a state legislature that becomes a law of general applicability.

summary judgment. A pretrial motion in which a party contends its opponent is not entitled to a jury trial because there are no factual issues in dispute to be resolved by a jury, and that the judge can decide the case as a matter of law.

T

termination. A cessation of employment, including a layoff, other than a voluntary resignation.

Title VII. That part of the *Civil Rights Act of 1964* that prohibits employment discrimination.

tort. A civil wrong of a noncontractual nature, such as assault, battery, defamation, or wrongful discharge.

trial. A formal court proceeding in which a factfinder, be it judge or jury, is called upon to decide which party is entitled to prevail after a full presentation of the evidence.

U

undue hardship. That level of hardship that makes a proposed accommodation unreasonable for an employer to bear.

V

verdict. A jury's decision.

W

Worker Adjustment and Retraining Act (WARN). A federal statute requiring notice to workers of plant closures and mass layoffs.

whistleblower laws. Laws that protect those who oppose illegal activity.

wrongful constructive discharge. A resignation induced by an employer under circumstances in which, had the person been terminated, the termination would have been unlawful.

wrongful discharge. A termination of employment under circumstances that makes it unlawful, such as for opposing illegal activity.

Appendix A

Frequently Asked Questions

Q: I know I am an employee at will.
Does that mean I have no right to sue if I am terminated?
No. All it means is that you can be terminated at any time without cause, for any reason except for an unlawful one. Unlawful reasons include those that violate a state's wrongful discharge law, based upon public policy, or a federal or state discrimination, retaliation, or whistleblowing statute. In addition, your termination could violate an enforceable agreement with your employer. (see Chapter 11.) Further, the manner in which you have been terminated may give rise to liability for other torts, for such things as invasion of privacy, defamation of character, or intentional infliction of emotional distress. (see Chapter 12.)

Q: I am a probationary employee—does that mean I have
no legal right to sue my employer if I am terminated?
No. Whether you work for a private employer or governmental body, if you are a probationary employee, you can sue your employer like any other employee at will under the same circumstances. During your probationary period, you still cannot be fired because of your protected class status (race, sex, age, etc.) or because of a reason that

has been recognized by the courts in your state as violative of public policy (such as for filing a workers' compensation claim or reporting illegal activity).

Q: *The document I signed says I am an independent contractor. Does that mean I have no legal protection against a wrongful discharge?*

Not necessarily. Whether you are or are not an employee does not depend on labels. An *economic realities* test is sometimes applied in cases brought under *Title VII*, the *ADEA*, and *ERISA*. Under those and the traditional common law test, the courts will look principally to whether the employer has the right to control the manner and means by which your work is accomplished.

In making that determination, the courts will look to factors such as:

- ✦ the skill required;
- ✦ which party furnishes the tools;
- ✦ the location of the work;
- ✦ the duration of the relationship between the parties;
- ✦ whether the hiring party has the right to assign additional projects to the hired party;
- ✦ the extent of the hired party's discretion over when and how long to work;
- ✦ the method of payment;
- ✦ the hired party's role in hiring and paying assistants;
- ✦ whether the work is part of the regular business of the hiring party;
- ✦ whether the hiring party is in business;
- ✦ whether employee benefits are provided; and,
- ✦ the tax treatment of the hired party.

Q: I am being harassed at work by my boss. Can I quit without losing my rights?

You may jeopardize some rights if you quit because of supervisor harassment. Supervisor harassment is a favorite tool of management to get rid of certain workers. Sometimes this method is used because of a worker's protected class status (race, sex, age, etc.) or because they have engaged in protected activity, such as filing a workers' compensation claim. It is also used when *cause* is required to discharge a worker, and the employee has done nothing wrong or has not done enough wrong.

Many—but not all—states have recognized the principle of *wrongful constructive discharge* in public policy wrongful discharge cases. Federal and most state discrimination laws recognize the principle as well. This means that if you quit under certain circumstances, your resignation will be treated as a wrongful discharge by the employer. Generally, however, this requires proof that you resigned because your employer maintained objectively intolerable working conditions because of your protected activity. When that is the case, the discharge is supplied as a legal construct or fiction. However, the test is an objective one. If you quit, you are taking the chance that a jury a year or two later will second-guess you and vote against you because it believes you should have held on a little longer or that the harassment was not severe enough.

Furthermore, you may place your unemployment compensation benefits in jeopardy by quitting. In some states, you forfeit those benefits if you voluntarily resign *without good cause*. Sometimes, without the complete discovery that is available in court proceedings, it is hard to prove *good cause* existed in the context of an informal administrative unemployment compensation hearing.

Consult an attorney before any resignation so you can obtain a professional assessment as to how close your situation comes in your state to meeting its wrongful constructive discharge proof requirements. (see Chapter 11.)

Q: I think they are going to fire me to replace me with a friend of the boss—is that illegal?

There is no law that prohibits a hiring preference based on friendship. However, a bias in favor of one's friends can open the door to discriminatory employment decisions that exclude members of a protected class. In every such case, you have the burden of proof of showing that you are disadvantaged because of your protected class status—such as race, sex, or age. Even so, the fact that you were disadvantaged merely because your boss wanted his or her friend in your place is not, itself, a wrongful termination.

Q: I think my boss wants to fire me because I know too much—is that illegal?

Most states recognize the public policy tort of wrongful discharge in which you can sue your employer if you are terminated in retaliation for engaging in what your state defines as *protected activity*, such as reporting to jury duty or reporting illegal activity. Currently, however, no state allows an employee to sue for wrongful discharge who has not engaged in protected activity, but was terminated merely because he or she knew too much. (see Chapter 11.)

Q: I am about to be terminated because my competence threatens my boss—is that illegal?

An employee at will can be terminated for any or no reason, except for one that violates a statute or public policy. No wrongful discharge claim for an at-will employee may be predicated upon a firing without cause, because none is required. Therefore, in a nonunion, private employer context, for an employer to terminate you because they are jealous of your competence, or are threatened by it, does not constitute wrongful discharge.

Q: I have just been terminated, but my boss will not tell me why—is that illegal?

Except in Indiana, Maine, Minnesota, and Missouri—where by statute an employer is required to give a terminated employee the reason for termination—it is not illegal for an employer to fire a worker and refuse to tell the worker why they are being fired. However, in most cases that does not occur because an employer that refuses to give a worker the reason for termination runs the risk the employee will think it unfair to withhold the justification for termination and cause the worker to seek out an attorney to review the matter.

Q: I was laid-off along with others. Does that mean I have no case?

No. The courts allow juries to look behind a nominal reorganization or layoff to see if it is merely being used as a smokescreen for a wrongful termination. If you were laid-off, but your job functions still need to be performed and they were assigned to others, your lawyer would examine why you were not allowed to continue to perform them yourself. Your supervisor would have to explain why that choice was made. Your supervisor's rationale would be tested. If your supervisor claimed your replacement was better qualified to perform your job, your qualifications and would be compared to your replacement's. Your layoff would be analyzed like any other wrongful termination case. (see Chapter 14.)

Q: My boss lied to me about why I was terminated. Is that illegal?

Except in the very few states where, by state statute, the employer is required to tell you in writing the *true* reason for your termination, to be lied to is not itself illegal. On the other hand, if you claim you were terminated because of your protected activity or protected class status, and are able to prove your employer's stated reason is false, that will greatly assist your case. If you disprove your employer's stated reason for termination, that will ordinarily raise an inference that the prohibited reason was the real reason for termination.

Q: If I am terminated, must I go through my union?

If you are a union member or are given protection under a union contract, and your collective bargaining agreement has a grievance mechanism that allows your particular dispute a hearing, the law is structured to strongly urge you to use that mechanism. If you do not, and your internal remedy was your exclusive remedy, you may be precluded from bringing a court suit.

Be aware of the extremely short deadlines under some union contracts for the filing of a grievance. Read the agreement yourself and speak with your union steward or business agent to get a clear understanding when those deadlines will occur. (see Chapter 13.)

Q: I lost my union grievance. Can I still pursue other legal remedies?

Even if your grievance went to arbitration and you lost, you may be able to pursue some nonunion court remedies. If your wrongful discharge case does not require interpretation of your collective bargaining agreement, you may be able to pursue that claim in court afterwards.

Other claims, such as those created by assault, battery, or defamation, may not relate at all to your union contract remedy. You may be able to pursue those other claims in court as well.

In some cases, you may be entitled to sue your union, your employer, or both in what is known as an *unfair representation case*, if your union failed to fulfill its duty of fair representation to you. They may do this by acting arbitrarily, capriciously, or in bad faith. Speak with a lawyer about whether you have legal remedies outside your union contract.

Q: When I was first hired I signed an agreement to arbitrate any employment dispute. Is that agreement valid?

Not necessarily. Even though the United States Supreme Court has held that employment agreements are subject to the *Federal Arbitration Act*, the enforceability of arbitration agreements are tested against the contract law of the state in which the agreements were made. The *Federal Arbitration Act* is designed to compel the resolution of legal disputes through arbitration. The Supreme Court has held that state law contract defenses, such as fraud, duress, or unconscionability, may be applied to invalidate arbitration agreements. Some arbitration agreements have been found to be unenforceable on grounds of *unconscionability*. The Supreme Court has also held that arbitration is enforceable only if the agreement preserves substantive state rights, such as the right to recover punitive damages (where those are available).

Two states have enacted statutes regulating the enforceability of arbitration agreements. In New Jersey, they are valid only if the arbitration clause is clear and unequivocal and specifically informs the employee of the waiver of statutory rights. Kentucky outlaws compulsory arbitration of employment agreements altogether. Obtain a lawyer's opinion as to the enforceability of any arbitration clause in your case.

Appendix B

Payment of Wages Upon Termination

This appendix lists the states that have statutes regulating the timing of the payment of wages upon termination.

ALASKA—Upon termination by employer, wages must be paid within three working days.

ARIZONA—Upon termination, wages must be paid the sooner of three working days or at end of next regular pay period.

CALIFORNIA—Upon termination by employer, wages must be paid immediately. Wages must be paid within seventy-two hours to those who quit.

COLORADO—Upon termination by employer, wages must be paid immediately, unless accounting unit is not then operational.

CONNECTICUT—If terminated, wages must be paid on next business day after discharge.

DELAWARE—If discharged by employer, employer must pay wages at next scheduled payday.

DISTRICT OF COLUMBIA—If discharged by employer, wages must be paid not later than next working day; quitting employee, upon earlier of next regular payday or within seven days.

HAWAII—If discharged, wages must be paid at the time of discharge, or if not possible, no later than the following day.

IDAHO—If terminated, at the next regular payday or within ten days of such termination, whichever is earlier.

ILLINOIS—Wages of separated worker must be paid in full at time of separation, if possible, but in no case later than next scheduled payday. Commissions must be paid within thirteen days of termination.

INDIANA—Upon termination, wages must be paid at next regular payday.

IOWA—Upon termination, wages are to be paid no later than next regular payday.

KANSAS—If discharged or quit, wages must be paid no later than next regular pay period.

KENTUCKY—If discharged, wages must be paid at next regular payday or within fourteen days, whichever is later.

LOUISIANA—Upon demand by employee after discharge or resignation, must pay wages within three days.

MAINE—If employee leaves employment, wages must be paid within defined reasonable time after demand.

MARYLAND—If discharged, wages must be paid at next regular payday.

MASSACHUSETTS—If discharged, must be paid upon date of discharge or, if in Boston, as soon as payroll laws are complied with, except that commissions may be paid when normally calculated. If resignation, wages must be paid by next regular payday or, if none, the following Saturday.

MICHIGAN—If quit or discharged, wages must be paid as soon as amount can be determined with due diligence.

MINNESOTA—Upon discharge, wages are payable immediately upon demand. If employee quits, wages are payable at next regular payday, unless within five days, then at following payday.

MISSOURI—If discharged, wages are due on the date of discharge.

MONTANA—Upon separation, wages must be paid at next regular payday or within fifteen days, whichever occurs first.

NEBRASKA—Upon termination, wages are payable at the next regular payday or within two weeks, whichever is sooner.

NEVADA—Discharged employee is entitled to payment of wages immediately, and employee who resigns is entitled the earlier of seven days or at next regular payday.

NEW HAMPSHIRE—Upon discharge, wages are due immediately and must be paid within seventy-two hours after demand, unless worker is employed at a place other than principal place of business, then at next regular pay day. If worker quits, wages due at next regular payday.

NEW JERSEY—Upon termination, wages due at next regular payday.

NEW MEXICO—If discharged, payment of wages within five days.

NEW YORK—If discharged, payment of wages by next regular payday.

NORTH CAROLINA—If employment is discontinued, payment of wages must be made by next regular payday, or if commission-based, after amount becomes calculable after separation.

NORTH DAKOTA—If discharged, payment of wages by next regular payday.

OKLAHOMA—Upon termination, employer must pay wages at next regular payday.

OREGON—If discharged, wages must be paid by end of first business day after discharge.

PENNSYLVANIA—If separated, payment of wages by next regular payday.

RHODE ISLAND—If discharged, wages must be paid on next regular payday, except in case of business closure, merger, liquidation, or out of state move, in which case payment is required within twenty-four hours.

SOUTH CAROLINA—If discharged, wages must be payed within forty-eight hours, or at next regular payday within thirty days.

SOUTH DAKOTA—If employee is discharged, wages must be paid within five days or as soon thereafter as employee returns to employer all property of the employer in employee's possession. If resigned, payment at next regular payday.

TENNESSEE—If employee quits or is dismissed, wages must be paid at next regular payday or within twenty-one days, whichever is later.

TEXAS—Discharged employee must be paid by sixth day after discharge. Employee who leaves for other reasons must be paid by next regular payday.

UTAH—Upon discharge, wages must be paid within twenty-four hours. Upon resignation, wages to be paid on next regular payday.

VERMONT—If discharged, payment of wages is within seventy-two hours. If employee resigned, it is on the last regular payday, or if there is no regular payday, the following Friday.

VIRGINIA—If terminated, payment of wages is at next regular payday.

WASHINGTON—If employee ceases to work for employer for any reason, payment of wages is at the end of established pay period.

WEST VIRGINIA—If discharged, wages must be paid within seventy-two hours.

WISCONSIN—If discharged, wages due at next regular payday.

WYOMING—If discharged or quits, employee must be paid within five working days.

Appendix C

Effect of Misconduct on Unemployment Benefits

This appendix lists the effect of termination for misconduct on state unemployment compensation benefits eligibility. (The disqualification period is in parentheses.)

ALABAMA—For misconduct unrelated with work (three to seven weeks). For actual or threatened deliberate misconduct in connection with work after repeated warnings (six to twelve weeks).

ALASKA— For misconduct in connection with work (six weeks). For felony or theft in connection with work (one year or until claimant earns twenty times weekly benefit).

ARIZONA—For willful or negligent misconduct connected with work (until claimant earns five times weekly benefit).

ARKANSAS—For misconduct connected with work (eight weeks). For gross misconduct (until reemployed for ten weeks and claimant earns ten times weekly benefit).

CALIFORNIA—For misconduct connected with most recent work (until claimant earns five times weekly benefit).

COLORADO—For statutory list of circumstances constituting misconduct—including, in part, insubordination, incarceration, theft, willful neglect, rudeness, careless work, refusal to work a different shift or transfer (no benefit will be paid).

CONNECTICUT—For felonious conduct, larceny, repeated willful misconduct in course of employment, just cause, or participation in an illegal strike (until claimant earns ten times weekly benefit).

DELAWARE—For just cause in connection with work (until reemployed for four weeks and claimant earns four times weekly benefit amount).

DISTRICT OF COLUMBIA—For misconduct (until reemployed for eight weeks and claimant earns eight times weekly benefit). For gross misconduct (until reemployed for ten weeks and claimant earns ten times weekly benefit).

FLORIDA—For misconduct connected with work (until reemployed and claimant earns seventeen times weekly benefit).

GEORGIA—For failure to obey orders, rules, or instructions, or failure to discharge duties (until reemployed and claimant earns ten times weekly benefit).

HAWAII—For misconduct (until claimant earns three times weekly benefit).

IDAHO—For misconduct connected with employment (until reemployed and claimant earns twelve times weekly benefit).

ILLINOIS—For misconduct (until reemployed and claimant earns four times weekly benefit). For felony or theft in connection with work, and admission or conviction (no benefit rights).

INDIANA—For just cause (until claimant earns eight times weekly benefit). For gross misconduct in connection with work, including felony or misdemeanor in connection with work, and admission or conviction (cancellation of all wage credits).

IOWA—For misconduct connected with work (until claimant earns ten times weekly benefit).

KANSAS—For misconduct connected with work (until reemployed and claimant earns three times weekly benefit).

KENTUCKY—For misconduct or dishonesty in connection with work (until reemployed ten weeks and claimant earns ten times weekly benefit).

LOUISIANA—For misconduct connected with work (until claimant earns ten times weekly benefit without subsequent disqualifying event).

MAINE—For misconduct connected with work (until claimant earns four times weekly benefit). For conviction of felony or misdemeanor in connection with work (until claimant earns the greater of $600 or eight times weekly benefit).

MARYLAND—For misconduct connected with work (five to ten weeks). For gross misconduct (until reemployed and claimant earns twenty times weekly benefit). For aggravated misconduct (until reemployed and claimant has earned thirty times weekly benefit).

MASSACHUSETTS—For deliberate misconduct in willful disregard of the employer's interest, due to a knowing violation of a reasonable and uniformly enforced rule or policy, or conviction of a felony or misdemeanor (until reemployed eight weeks and claimant has earned amount equal to weekly benefit in each week during that period).

MICHIGAN—For misconduct connected with work, or intoxication at work (until claimant earns lesser of seven times weekly benefit or forty times minimum hourly wage times seven). If in connection with work, for assault and battery, theft, or willful destruction of property (thirteen requalification weeks).

MINNESOTA—For misconduct (until claimant earns eight times weekly benefit). For gross misconduct (until claimant earns twelve times weekly benefit).

MISSISSIPPI—For misconduct connected with work (until claimant earns eight times weekly benefit).

MISSOURI—For misconduct connected with work (four to sixteen weeks).

MONTANA—For misconduct connected with work (until claimant earns eight times weekly benefit). For gross misconduct connected with work (fifty-two weeks).

NEBRASKA—For misconduct connected with work (for a total of eight to eleven weeks). For gross, flagrant, and willful misconduct, or conduct that was unlawful (cancellation of wage credits).

NEVADA—For misconduct connected with work (two to sixteen weeks). For commission of assault, arson, sabotage, larceny, embezzlement, or destruction of property in connection with work, and admission or conviction (no benefits).

NEW HAMPSHIRE—For misconduct (until claimant earns 120% of weekly benefit in each of five weeks). For arson, sabotage, commission of a felony, or dishonesty (loss of all wage credits). For intoxication or use of controlled drugs (four to twenty-six weeks).

NEW JERSEY—For misconduct connected with work (six weeks). For gross misconduct connected with work (until reemployed four weeks and claimant earns six times weekly benefit).

NEW MEXICO—For misconduct connected with work (until reemployed and claimant earns five times weekly benefit).

NEW YORK—For misconduct connected with work (until claimant earns five times weekly benefit).

NORTH CAROLINA—For misconduct connected with work (duration of unemployment, and until reemployed five weeks and claimant earns ten times weekly benefit).

NORTH DAKOTA—For misconduct connected with work (until claimant earns ten times weekly benefit). If for gross misconduct (one year).

OHIO—For just cause (duration of unemployment).

OKLAHOMA—For misconduct connected with work (until claimant earns ten times weekly benefit).

OREGON—For misconduct connected with work (until claimant earns four times weekly benefit).

PENNSYLVANIA—For willful misconduct connected with work (until claimant earns six times weekly benefit).

RHODE ISLAND—For misconduct connected with work (until claimant earns eight times weekly benefit).

SOUTH CAROLINA—For cause connected with work (six to twenty-six weeks).

SOUTH DAKOTA—For misconduct (until reemployed at least six weeks and in each earns amount equal to weekly benefit).

TENNESSEE—For misconduct connected with work (until reemployed and claimant earns ten times weekly benefit).

TEXAS—For misconduct connected with last work (until reemployed six weeks or claimant earns six times weekly benefit).

UTAH—For just cause due to misconduct connected with work (until claimant earns six times weekly benefit). For dishonesty constituting a crime, or any felony or class A misdemeanor (fifty-two weeks and loss of wage credits).

VERMONT—For misconduct (six to twelve weeks). For gross misconduct (until claimant reemployed and earns six times weekly benefit).

VIRGINIA—For misconduct connected with work (until after reemployed thirty days or 240 hours and subsequently separated).

WASHINGTON—For misconduct connected with work (seven weeks, and until reemployed and claimant earns seven times weekly benefit). If felony or gross misdemeanor connected with work, and admission or conviction (all wage credits cancelled).

WEST VIRGINIA—For misconduct (a total of seven weeks).

WISCONSIN—For misconduct connected with work (seven weeks and claimant earns fourteen times weekly benefit).

WYOMING—For misconduct connected with most recent work (until reemployed twelve weeks and claimant earns twelve times weekly benefit amount).

Appendix D

State Discrimination Laws and Agencies

There are many differences from state to state in the content of state discrimination laws. Listed here, in alphabetical order, is a description of the discrimination laws of each state and the District of Columbia. Also listed is information on how to reach your state discrimination enforcement agency (if you have one) for questions or claim filings.

ALABAMA

LAW—Prohibits discrimination against employees 40 years and over on the basis of age. (Ala. Code Secs. 25-1-20 and following.) There is no statutory provision regarding discrimination on the basis of race, color, religion, sex, national origin or disability, except in state employment.

AGENCY—There is no state civil rights agency.

ALASKA

LAW—Prohibits discrimination because of race, religion, color, national origin, age, sex, physical or mental disability, marital status, pregnancy, or parenthood, where reasonable demands of position do not require distinction. (Alaska Stat. Secs. 18.80.010 and following.)

AGENCY—Alaska State Commission for Human Rights
        800 A Street
        Suite 204
        Anchorage, Alaska 99501-3669
        907-276-7474

ARIZONA

LAW—Prohibits discrimination on basis of race, color, religion, sex, results of a genetic test, handicap, national origin, or age. (Ariz. Rev. Stat. Secs. 41-1461 and following.)

AGENCY—Arizona Civil Rights Division
        Office of Arizona Attorney General
        1275 W. Washington Street
        Phoenix, Arizona 85007-2926
        602-542-5263

ARKANSAS

LAW—Prohibits discrimination on basis of race, religion, ancestry, national origin, gender, or sensory, mental or physical disability. (Ark. Code Ann. Secs. 16-123-102 and following.)

AGENCY—Equal Employment Opportunity Commission
        Little Rock Area Office
        425 W. Capitol Avenue
        Suite 625
        Little Rock, Arkansas 72201
        501-324-5060

CALIFORNIA

LAW—Prohibits discrimination on basis of race, religious creed, color, national origin, ancestry, physical or mental disability, medical condition related to a history or diagnosis of cancer or to genetic characteristics, marital status, sex, age, or sexual orientation. (Cal. Govt C. Sec. 12940.)

AGENCY—California Department of Fair Employment and Housing
2014 T Street
Suite 210
Sacramento, CA 95814 5212
916-227-2873

COLORADO

LAW—Prohibits discrimination on basis of disability, race, creed, color, sex, age, national origin, ancestry. (Colo. Rev. Stat. Sec. 24-34-402.) Makes unlawful termination for engaging in lawful activity off employer's premises, unless restriction relates to a bona fide occupational requirement, is reasonably and rationally related to employment activities and responsibilities of a particular employee or employee group, or is necessary to avoid conflict of interest or appearance thereof. (Colo. Rev. Stat. Sec. 24-34-402.5.)

AGENCY—Colorado Civil Rights Division Commission
1560 Broadway
Suite 1050
Denver, Colorado 80202-5143
303-894-2997

CONNECTICUT

LAW—Prohibits discrimination on basis of race, color, religious creed, age, sex, marital status, national origin, ancestry, present or past history of mental disability, mental retardation, learning disability or physical disability, genetic information, or sexual orientation. (Conn. Gen. Stat. Secs. 46a - 60 and following.)

AGENCY—Connecticut Commission on Human Rights and
Opportunities
21 Grand Street
Hartford, Connecticut 06106
860-541-3400

DELAWARE

LAW—Prohibits discrimination on basis of race, marital status, genetic information, color, age, religion, sex, or national origin. (Del. Code Ann Tit. 19, Sec. 711.)

AGENCY—Delaware Department of Labor
　　　　　Office of Labor Law Enforcement
　　　　　4425 N. Market Street
　　　　　Washington, Delaware 19802
　　　　　302-761-8200, ext. 3

DISTRICT OF COLUMBIA

LAW—Prohibits discrimination on basis of actual or perceived race, color, religion, national origin, sex, age, marital status, personal appearance, sexual orientation, familial status, family responsibilities, disability, matriculation, or political affiliation.
(D.C. Code Sec. 2-1402.11.)

AGENCY—Department of Human Rights & Minority Business
　　　　　Development
　　　　　441 4th Street, NW
　　　　　Suite 570 North
　　　　　Washington, DC 20001
　　　　　202-727-4559

FLORIDA

LAW—Prohibits discrimination on basis of race, color, religion, sex, national origin, age, handicap, or marital status.
(Fla. Stat. Sec. 760.01.)

AGENCY—Florida Commission on Human Relations
　　　　　2009 Apalachee Parkway
　　　　　Suite 100
　　　　　Tallahassee, Florida 32301
　　　　　850-488-7082

GEORGIA

LAW—Prohibits discrimination on basis of sex, (Ga. Code Ann Sec. 34-5-1), age (40-70) (Ga. Code Ann Sec. 34-1-2), handicap (Ga. Code Ann Sec. 34-6A-1 and following), attendance at a judicial proceeding except where employee is charged with a crime. (Ga. Code Ann Sec. 34-1-3.) Also prohibits discrimination in public employment on basis of race, color, religion, national origin, sex, handicap, or age. (40-70). (Ga. Code Ann Sec. 45-19-29.)

AGENCY—Georgia Commission on Equal Opportunity
229 Peachtree Street NE
Suite 710, International Tower
Atlanta, Georgia 30303-1605
404-656-1736

HAWAII

LAW—Prohibits discrimination on basis of race, sex, sexual orientation, age, religion, color, ancestry, disability, marital status, or arrest and court record not rationally related to job. Also prohibits discrimination against lactating employee who breastfeeds or expresses milk during meal or break period. (Haw. Rev. Stat. Sec. 378-10-2.) Prohibits discrimination solely on ground employer is summoned as garnishee for employee's debt, or because of work injury compensable under workers' compensation law.
(Haw. Rev. Stat. Sec. 378-32.)

AGENCY—Hawaii Civil Rights Commission
830 Punchbowl Street
Room 411
Honolulu, Hawaii 96813
808-586-8636

IDAHO

LAW—Prohibits discrimination on the basis of race, color, religion, sex, national origin, age (40 and over) or disability.
(Idaho Code Sec. 67-5909.)

AGENCY—Idaho Human Rights Commission
P.O. Box 83720
1109 Main Street
Suite 400
Boise, Idaho 83720-0040
208-334-2873

ILLINOIS

LAW—Prohibits discrimination on basis of race, color, religion, national origin, ancestry, age (40 to 70), sex, marital status, physical or mental handicap, military status, or unfavorable discharge except for dishonorable discharge. (775 ILCS 5/1-102 and following.)

AGENCY—Illinois Human Rights Commission
James R. Thompson Center
100 W. Randolph Street
Suite 5-100
Chicago, Illinois 60601
312-814-6269
or
William G. Stratton Office Building
Room 404
Springfield, Illinois 62706
217-785-4350

INDIANA
LAW—Prohibits discrimination on basis of race, religion, color, sex, disability, national origin, ancestry, and age (40-70). (Ind. Code Sec. 22-9-1-1 and following.)
AGENCY—Indiana Civil Rights Commission
Indiana Government Center
100 N. Senate Avenue
Room 103
Indianapolis, Indiana 46204
317-232-2600

IOWA
LAW—Prohibits discrimination on basis of age, race, creed, color, sex, national origin, religion, or disability. (Iowa Code Sec. 216.6.)
AGENCY—Iowa Civil Rights Commission
Ginmes State Office Building
400 E 14th Street
Des Moines, Iowa 50319-1004
515-281-4121

KANSAS
LAW—Prohibits discrimination on basis of race, religion, color, sex, disability, national origin or ancestry, without business necessity. (Kan. Stat. Ann. Sec. 44-1009.) Age discrim-

ination for reasons of age 18 or more is prohibited unless a valid business motive exists, except that executives may be forced to retire at age 65 if they will receive at least $44,000 per year in retirement benefits. (Kan. Stat. Ann. Secs. 44-1113 and 1118.)

AGENCY—Kansas Human Rights Commission
        900 SW Jackson
        Suite 851-S
        Landon State Office Building
        Topeka, Kansas 66612 1258
        785-296-3206

KENTUCKY

LAW—Prohibits discrimination on basis of race, color, religion, national origin, sex, disability, age (40 and over), or because the person is a smoker or non-smoker so long as the person complies with any workplace policy concerning smoking.
(Ky. Rev. Stat. Ann. Secs. 344.030 and following.)

AGENCY—Kentucky Commission on Human Rights
        332 W. Broadway
        Suite 700
        Louisville, Kentucky 40202
        502-595-4024

LOUISIANA

LAW—Prohibits discrimination on basis of age (40 and over), race, color, religion, pregnancy, childbirth, and related medical conditions, disability, protected genetic information, sex, and national origin. (La. Rev. Stat. Ann. 23:301 and following.)

AGENCY—Louisiana Commission on Human Rights
        1001 N. 23rd Street
        Baton Rouge, LA 70802
        225-342-6969

MAINE

LAW—Prohibits discrimination on basis of race, color, sex, physical or mental disability, religion, age, ancestry, or national origin, for previous assertion of claim or right under workers' compensation laws, or for previous activity under state Whistleblower's Protection Act. Also prohibits discrimination on the basis of sexual preference. (Me. Rev. Stat. Ann. Tit..5, Sec. 4553 (10-g).)

AGENCY—Maine Human Rights Commission
   State House—Station 51
   Augusta, Maine 04333-0051
   207-624-6050

MARYLAND

LAW—Prohibits discrimination on basis of race, color, religion, sex, age, national origin, marital status, genetic information, sexual orientation, physical or mental disability unrelated in nature and extent so as to reasonably preclude performance of employment for refusing to submit to a genetic test or make available the results of a genetic test, or for opposing any unlawful practice or participation in proceeding. (Md. Ann. Code Art. 49B, Sec. 16.)

AGENCY—Maryland Commission on Human Relations
   6 St. Paul Street
   Suite 900
   Baltimore, Maryland 21202-2274
   410-767-8600

MASSACHUSETTS

LAW—Prohibits discrimination on basis of race, color, religious creed, national origin, sex, sexual orientation, which shall not include persons whose sexual orientation involves minor children as the sex object, genetic information, ancestry, age (40 and over), handicap, or membership in labor unions. (Mass. Gen. Laws Ch. 151 B, Sec. 4 and following.) Also prohibits discrimination against persons refusing to provide information regarding arrests not leading to conviction, and first convictions for certain violations and misdemeanors. (Sec. 4 [9].) Also prohibits discrimination against persons who failed to inform of commitment to mental institution, provided person has been discharged and has psychiatric certification of mental competence. (Sec. 4 [9A].) Also prohibits discrimination against person who opposed practices forbidden by civil rights laws. (Sec 34 [4]) or who aid or encourage any other person to exercise civil rights. (Sec. 4 [4A].) Also prohibits discrimination on basis of political activity. (Mass. Gen. Laws Ch 56, sec. 33.)

AGENCY—Massachusetts Commission Against
             Discrimination
             Ashburton Place
             Room 601
             Boston, Massachusetts 02108-1518
             617-994-6000

MICHIGAN

LAW—Prohibits discrimination on basis of religion, race, color, national origin, sex, age, height, weight, or marital status. (Mich. Comp. Laws Secs. 37.2101 and following.) Also prohibits discrimination because of disability or genetic condition unrelated to ability to perform work. (Mich. Comp. Laws Secs. 37.1101 and following.)

AGENCY—Michigan Department of Civil Rights
             Capitol Tower Building
             Suite 800
             Lansing, Michigan 48933
             517-335-3165

MINNESOTA

LAW—Prohibits discrimination on basis of race, color, religious creed, national origin, sex, marital status, status with regard to public assistance, membership or activity in any anti-discrimination agency, disability, sexual orientation, age (over 25). (Minn. Stat. Secs. 363.01 and following.) Also prohibits discrimination for not contributing to charity or community organization. (Minn. Stat. Sec. 181.937.) Also prohibits discrimination for lawful use of consumable products off employer's premises during working hours. (Minn. Stat. Sec. 181.938.) Also prohibits discrimination for certain whistle blowing activities. (Minn. Stat. Secs. 181.932 and 181.935.)

AGENCY—Minnesota Department of Human Rights
Army Corps of Engineers Centre
190 E. 5ᵗʰ Street
Suite 700
St. Paul, Minnesota 55101
651-296-5663

MISSISSIPPI

LAW—Does not regulate private employers. Prohibits discrimination in state employment on basis of race, color, religion, sex, national origin, age, or handicap. (Miss. Code Ann. Sec. 25-9-149.)

AGENCY—There is no state civil rights agency.

MISSOURI

LAW—Prohibits employers of more than six persons from discriminating on basis of race, color, religion, national origin, sex, ancestry, age (40-70), or disability. (Mo. Rev. Stat. Secs. 213.010 and following.)

AGENCY—Missouri Commission on Human Rights
3315 W. Truman Boulevard
Jefferson City, Missouri 65012-1129
573-751-4091

MONTANA

LAW—Prohibits discrimination on the basis of race, creed, religion, color, national origin, age, physical or mental disability, marital states or sex, when the reasonable demands of the position do not require an age, physical or mental disability, marital status, or sex distinction. (Mont. Code Ann. Sec. 49-2-303.)

AGENCY—Montana Human Rights Commission
P.O. Box 1222
Helena, Montana 59624
Tel 406-444-2884

NEBRASKA

LAW—Prohibits discrimination on basis of race, color, religion, sex, age (40-70), disability, marital status, or national origin. (Neb. Rev. Stat. Secs. 48-1101 and following.)

AGENCY—Nebraska Equal Opportunity Commission
        State Office Building
        301 Centennial Mall South
        5th Floor
        P.O. Box 94934
        Lincoln, Nebraska 68509-4934
        402-471-2024

NEVADA

LAW—Prohibits discrimination because of race, color, religion, sex, sexual orientation, age, disability, or national origin. (Nev. Rev. Stat. Sec. 613.330.)

AGENCY—Nevada Equal Rights Commission
        1515 E. Tropicana Avenue
        Suite 590
        Las Vegas, Nevada 89119-6522
        702-486-7161

NEW HAMPSHIRE

LAW—Prohibits discrimination on basis of age, sex, race, color, marital status, physical or mental disability, religious creed, national origin, or sexual orientation. (N.H. Rev. Stat. Ann. Sec. 354-A:7.)

AGENCY—New Hampshire Commission For Human Rights
        2 Chenelle Drive
        Concord, New Hampshire 03301-8501
        603-271-2767

NEW JERSEY

LAW—Prohibits discrimination on basis of race, creed, color, national origin, ancestry, age, marital status, affectional or sexual orientation, genetic information, sex, or atypical cellular or blood trait, disability for military service, nationality, refusal to submit to genetic tests or to make results available to employer, and age (to 70). (N.J. Stat. Ann. Sec. 10:5-12.) Also under Conscientious Employee Protection Act, prohibits discrimination against employee who discloses or threatens to disclose to supervisor or public body activity, policy or practice or employer, co-employee or another employee with whom employer has a business relationship, that employee objectively reasonably believes violated law, testifies about any such violation, or objects to or refuses to participate in such activity, or one that is fraudulent or criminal, or incompatible with clear mandate of public policy concerning health, safety, welfare, or protection of the environment. (N.J. Stat. Ann. Sec. 34:19-3.) Requires employee to first bring notice of such activity, policy, or practice to attention of supervisor in writing, except in certain circumstances, including reasonable fear of personal safety. (N.J. Stat. Ann. Sec. 34:19-3.)

AGENCY—New Jersey Department of Laws and Safety
    Divisions of Civil Rights
    31 Clinton Street
    P.O. Box 40001
    Newark, New Jersey 07102
    973-648-2720

NEW MEXICO

LAW—Prohibits discrimination by reason of race, age, religion, color, national origin, ancestry, sex, spousal affiliation, physical or mental handicap or serious medical condition.
    (N.M. Stat. Ann. Secs. 28-1-7 and following.)

AGENCY—New Mexico Human Rights Commission
    New Mexico Department of Labor Education Bureau
    1596 Pacheco Street
    Suite 103
    Santa Fe, New Mexico 87505
    505-827-6838

NEW YORK

LAW—Prohibits discrimination because of age, race, creed, color, national origin, sexual orientation, sex, disability, genetic predispositions or carrier status, or marital status. (N.Y. Exec. Law Sec. 296.)

AGENCY—New York State Division of Human Rights
    One Fordham Plaza
    4th Floor
    Bronx, New York 10458
    718-741-8400

NORTH CAROLINA

LAW—Prohibits discrimination on account of race, religion, color, national origin, age, sex, or handicap or disability. (N.C. Gen. Stat. Sec. 143-422.2.) Also prohibits retaliation for filing complaint under Workers' Compensation Act, or Wage and Hour Act, or Office Safety and Health Act or Occupational Safety and Health Act. (N.C. Gen. Stat. Sec. 95-196.) Also prohibits discrimination based on genetic testing or genetic information. (N.C. Gen. Stat. Sec. 95-196.) Also prohibits discrimination against persons who have complied with court ordered parental duties under juvenile code. (N.C. Gen. Stat. Sec. 95-241.) Also prohibits discrimination against persons using lawful products during non-working hours, except that employer can restrict use if related to bona fide occupational requirements, fundamental objectives of organization, or violates substance abuse prevention programs. (N.C. Gen. Stat. Sec. 95-28.2.) Also prohibits discrimination against military personnel. (N.C. Gen. Stat. Sec. 127B-10-12.) Also prohibits discrimination for taking leave up to four hours annually to participate in or attend activities at child's school. (N.C. Gen. Stat. Sec. 95-28.3.) Also prohibits discrimination against persons having AIDS or HIV infection in determining suitability for continued employment, but not prohibited to deny employment to job applicant based on confirmed positive test for AIDS virus infection. (N.C. Gen. Stat. Sec. 130A-148[i].)

AGENCY—North Carolina Human Relations Commission
    217 W. Jones Street
    4th Floor
    Raleigh, North Carolina 27603-1336
    Tel 919-733-7996
    or
    North Carolina Human Relations Commission
    1318 Mail Service Center
    Raleigh, North Carolina 27699
    919-733-7996

NORTH DAKOTA

LAW—Prohibits discrimination because of race, color, religion, sex, national origin, age, physical or mental disability, marital status, receipt of public assistance, or participation in lawful activity off employer's premises during nonworking hours which is not in direct conflict with essential business-related interest of employer. (N.D. Cent. Code Sec. 14-02.4-03.)

AGENCY—North Dakota Department of Labor
600 E. Boulevard Avenue
Department 406
Bismarck, North Dakota 58505-0340
701-328-2660

OHIO

LAW—Prohibits discrimination on basis of race, color, religion, sex, national origin, disability, age or ancestry. (Ohio Rev. Code Ann. Sec. 4112.02.) Also prohibits discrimination against those who file or pursue workers' compensation claims.
(Ohio Rev. Code Ann. Sec. 4123.90.)

AGENCY—Ohio Civil Rights Commission
1111 E. Broad Street
Suite 301
Columbus, Ohio 43205-1379
614-466-2785

OKLAHOMA

LAW—Prohibits discrimination on basis of race, color, religion, sex, national origin, age, or handicap, unless action is related to a bona fide occupational qualification reasonably necessary to the normal operation of the employer's business or enterprise. (Okla. Stat. Tit. 25, Sec. 1302.) Act specifically does not require preferential treatment of individual or group on account of imbalance with respect to total number or percentage of persons of any group. (Okla. Stat. Tit. 25, Sec. 1310.)

AGENCY—Oklahoma Human Rights Commission
2101 N. Lincoln Boulevard
Room 480
Oklahoma City, Oklahoma 73105
405-521-2360

OREGON

LAW—Prohibits discrimination on basis of race, religion, color, sex, national origin, marital status, age (18 or older) or the race, religion, color, sex, national origin, marital status, or age of any other person with whom the person associates, or because of an expunged juvenile record, or disability. (Or. Rev. Stat. Sec. 659A.030.) Also prohibits retaliation against persons for making safety complaints (Or. Rev. Stat. Sec. 654.062), making complaints about health care facilities, testifying in good faith in unemployment compensation hearings (Or. Rev. Stat. Sec. 659A.035), giving legislative testimony (Or. Rev. Stat. Sec. 659A.270), for whistleblowing (Or. Rev. Stat. Sec. 659A.505 and 659A.550), for performing jury service (Or. Rev. Stat. Sec.10.090), solely because certain persons related by blood or marriage works or has worked for the company (Or. Rev. Stat. Sec. 659A.340), because the person filed a workers' compensation claim (Or. Rev. Stat. Sec.659A.410), or has made a wage claim. (Or. Rev. Stat. Sec. 652.355.)

AGENCY—Oregon Bureau of Labor and Industries Civil Right Division
800 NE Oregon
Suite 1070
Portland, Oregon 97232
503-731-4075

PENNSYLVANIA

LAW—Prohibits discrimination because of race, color, religious creed, ancestry, age, sex, national origin, non-job related handicap or disability, or use of a guide dog or support animal. (P. Stat. Ann. Tit. 43, Sec. 955.)

AGENCY—Pennsylvania Human Relations Commission
301 Chestnut Street
Suite 300
Harrisburg, Pennsylvania 17105
717-787-4087

RHODE ISLAND

LAW—Prohibits discrimination on basis of race, color, religion, disability, age (40-70), sexual orientation, gender identity or
expression, or country of ancestral origin. (R.I. Gen. Laws Sec.
28-5-7.) Also prohibits discrimination for engaging in or planning to engage in whistleblowing activity concerning a violation or prospective violation of law or regulation.
(R.I. Gen. Laws Sec. 28-49-1.3.)
AGENCY—Rhode Island Commission For Human Rights
180 Westminster Street
3rd Floor
Providence, Rhode Island 02903-3768
401-222-2661

SOUTH CAROLINA

LAW—Prohibits discrimination on basis of race, religion, color, sex,
age, national origin, or disability. (S.C. Code Ann. Sec. 1-13-80.)
Also prohibits discrimination against employee who complies
with valid subpoena to testify in court or administrative proceeding, or for institution or participating in workers' compensation
actions. (S.C. Code Ann. Sec. 41-1-80.)
AGENCY—South Carolina Human Rights Commission
2611 Forest Drive
Suite 200
P.O. Box 4490
Columbus, South Carolina 29204-4490
803-737-7800

SOUTH DAKOTA

LAW—Prohibits discrimination on basis of race, color, creed, religion, sex, ancestry, disability, national origin.
(S.D. Codified Laws Secs. 20-13-1 and following.)
AGENCY—South Dakota Division of Human Rights
700 Governors Drive
Pierre, South Dakota 57501
605-773-4493

TENNESSEE

LAW—Prohibits discrimination on basis of race, creed, color, religion, sex, age, or national origin. (Tenn. Code Ann. Sec. 4-21-401.) Also prohibits discrimination solely on basis of a physical, mental, or visual handicap and makes violation a Class C misdemeanor. (Tenn. Code Ann. Sec. 8-50-103.)
AGENCY—Tennessee Human Rights Commission
530 Church Street
Suite 400
Nashville, Tennessee 37243-0745
615-741-5825

TEXAS

LAW—Prohibits discrimination on basis of race, color, disability, religion, sex, national origin, or age. (Tex. Lab. Code Ann. Sec. 21.051.) Also prohibits discrimination for participating in public evacuation (Tex. Lab. Code Ann. Sec. 22.002), for participating in a strike (Tex. Lab. Code Ann. Sec. 52.031) or against persons who in good faith filed a workers' compensation claim, hired a lawyer for representation in such a claim, or instituted or testified in a workers' compensation proceeding.
(Tex. Lab. Code Ann. Sec. 451.001 to .003.)

AGENCY—Texas Commission on Human Rights
6330 Highway 290 East
Suite 250
Austin, Texas 78723
or
P. O. Box 13006
Austin, Texas 78711
512-437-3450

UTAH

LAW—Prohibits discrimination because of race, color, sex, pregnancy, childbirth, pregnancy related conditions, age (40 or over), religion, national origin, or disability.
(Utah Code Ann. Sec. 34A-5-106.)

AGENCY—Utah Anti-Discrimination Division
160 East 300 South
3rd Floor
Salt Lake City, Utah 84114-6640
or
P.O. Box 146630
Salt Lake City, Utah 84114
801-530-6801

VERMONT

LAW—Prohibits discrimination on the basis of race, color, religion, ancestry, national origin, sex, sexual orientation, place of birth, age, or disability. (Vt. Stat. Ann. Tit. 21, Sec. 495.)

AGENCY—Vermont Human Rights Commission
135 State Street
Drawer 33
Montpelier, Vermont 05633-6301
802-828-2480

VIRGINIA

LAW—Prohibits discrimination on basis of race, color, religion, national origin, sex, pregnancy, childbirth or related medical conditions, age (40 and over), marital status, or disability. (Va. Code Ann. Sec. 2.2 3900.)

AGENCY—Virginia Council on Human Rights
        900 E. Main Street
        Pocahontas Building
        4th Floor
        Richmond, Virginia 23219
        804-225-2292

WASHINGTON

LAW—Prohibits discrimination basis of age (40 and over), sex, marital status, race, creed, color, national origin, presence of sensory, mental, or physical disability, or the use of a dog guide or service animal by a disabled person. (Wash. Rev. Code Sec. 49.60.180.) Also prohibits discrimination on basis of HIV test results, unless absence of HIV is bona fide occupational qualification. (Wash. Rev. Code Sec. 49.60.172-.210.)

AGENCY—Washington State Human Rights Commission
        711 S. Capitol Way
        Suite 402
        Olympia, Washington 98504-2490
        360-753-6770

WEST VIRGINIA

LAW—Prohibits discrimination on basis of race, religion, color, national origin, ancestry, sex, age (40 or over), blindness or disability. (W. Va. Code Sec. 5-11-9.) Also prohibits discrimination for employee receiving or attempting to receive workers' compensation benefits. (W. Va. Code Sec. 23-5A-1.) Also prohibits discharge of worker off work due to compensable injury, except where employee committed separate dischargeable offense. (W. Va. Code Sec. 23-5A-3.)

AGENCY—West Virginia Human Rights Commission
        1321 Plaza East
        Room 108 A
        Charleston, West Virginia 25301-1400
        304-558-2616

WISCONSIN

LAW—Prohibits discrimination by reason of age (40 and over), race, creed, color, disability, marital status, sex, national origin, ancestry, arrest or conviction record, membership in national guard or military, or use or non-use of lawful products off employer's premises during non-working hours. (Wis. Stat. Sec. 111.321.) Also prohibits discrimination because of sexual orientation. (Wis. Stat. Sec. 111.36.) Also prohibits discrimination against person for attempting to enforce statutory right, opposing discriminating practice, making complaint, or aiding or testifying in proceeding. (Wis. Stat. Sec. 111.322.) Exception to age discrimination provided to allow age distinction where knowledge or experience to be gained is required for future advancement to arrangement or executive positions, or where employee is exposed to physical danger or hazards, such as certain employment in law enforcement or fire fighting. (Wis. Stat. Sec. 111.33.)

AGENCY—Wisconsin Equal Rights Division, Civil Rights Bureau
        201 East Washington Avenue
        Room A300
        P.O. Box 8928
        Madison, Wisconsin 53708-8928
        608-266-6860

WYOMING

LAW—Prohibits discrimination because of age (40-70), sex, race, creed, color, national origin, ancestry, or disability.
(Wyo. Stat. Ann. Sec. 27-9-105.)

AGENCY—Wyoming Department of Employment/Fair Hiring
        Programs
        1510 E. Pershing Boulevard
        West Wing
        Cheyenne, Wyoming 82002
        307-777-7261

Appendix E

EEOC Office Directory

The *Equal Employment Opportunity Commission (EEOC)* is the federal agency charged with receiving most federally-based administrative complaints of discrimination, including those for race, color, national origin, religion, sex, age, and disability. You may be able to make a joint federal and state filing through your state civil rights enforcement agency, if your state has one.

This appendix provides information on how to reach your regional EEOC office directly.

HEADQUARTERS
U.S. Equal Employment Opportunity Commission
1801 L Street, N.W.
Suite 100
Washington, DC 20507
202-419-0713

FIELD OFFICES
To be automatically connected with the nearest EEOC field office, call 800-669-4000

Albuquerque District Office
505 Marquette Street, N.W.
Suite 900
Albuquerque, NM 87102
505-248-5201

Atlanta District Office
Sam Nunn Atlanta Federal Center
100 Alabama Street, S.W.
Suite 4R30
Atlanta, GA 30303
404-562-6800

Baltimore District Office
City Crescent Building
10 South Howard Street
3rd Floor
Baltimore, MD 21201
410-962-3932

Birmingham District Office
Ridge Park Place
1130 22nd Street
Suite 2000
Birmingham, AL 32205
205-212-2100

Boston Area Office
John F. Kennedy Federal Building
Government Center
4th Floor, Room 475
Boston, MA 02203
617-565-3200

Buffalo Local Office
6 Fountain Plaza
Suite 350
Buffalo, NY 14202
716-551-4441

Charlotte District Office
129 West Trade Street
Suite 400
Charlotte, NC 28202
704-344-6682

Chicago District Office
500 West Madison Street
Suite 2800
Chicago, IL 60661
312-353-2713

Cincinnati Area Office
John W. Peck Federal
  Office Building
550 Main Street
10th Floor
Cincinnati, OH 45202
513-684-2851

Cleveland District Office
Tower City—
  Skylight Office Tower
1660 West Second Street
Suite 850
Cleveland, OH 44113-1454
216-522-2003

Dallas District Office
207 S. Houston Street
3rd Floor
Dallas, TX 75202-4726
214-253-2700

Denver District Office
303 E. 17th Avenue
Suite 510
Denver, CO 80203
303-866-1300

Detroit District Office
Patrick V. McNamara Building
477 Michigan Avenue
Room 865
Detroit, MI 48226-9704
313-226-4600

El Paso Area Office
300 East Main Street
El Paso, TX 79901
915-534-6700

Fresno Local Office
1265 West Shaw Avenue
Suite 103
Fresno, CA 93711
559-487-5793

Greensboro Local Office
2303 W. Meadow View Road
Suite 201
Greensboro, NC 27407
336-547-4188

Greenville Local Office
301 North Main Street
Suite 1402
Greenville, SC 29601-9916
864-241-4400

Honolulu Local Office
300 Ala Moana Boulevard
Room 7127
P.O. Box 50082
Honolulu, HI 96850-0051
808-541-3120

Houston District Office
Mickey Leland Federal Building
1919 Smith Street
Suites 600 and 700
Houston, TX 77002-8049
713-209-3320

Indianapolis District Office
101 West Ohio Street
Suite 1900
Indianapolis, IN 46204-4203
317-226-7212

Jackson Area Office
Dr. A.H. McCoy Federal Building
100 West Capitol Street
Suite 207
Jackson, MS 39269
601-965-4537

Kansas City Area Office
Gateway Tower II
4th and State Avenues
9th Floor
Kansas City, KS 66101
913-551-5655

Little Rock Area Office
820 Louisiana Street
Suite 200
Little Rock, AR 72201
501-324-5060

Los Angeles District Office
Roybal Federal Building
255 East Temple Street
4th Floor
Los Angeles, CA 90012
213-894-1000

Louisville Area Office
600 Dr. Martin Luther King Jr.
   Place
Suite 268
Louisville, KY 40202
502-582-6082

Memphis District Office
1407 Union Avenue
Suite 521
Memphis, TN 38104
901-544-0115

Miami District Office
One Biscayne Tower
2 South Biscayne Boulevard
Suite 2700
Miami, FL 33131
305-536-4491

Milwaukee District Office
Reuss Federal Plaza
310 West Wisconsin Avenue
Suite 800
Milwaukee, WI 53203-2292
414-297-1111

Minneapolis Area Office
Towle Building
330 South Second Avenue
Suite 430
Minneapolis, MN 55401-2224
612-335-4040

Nashville Area Office
50 Vantage Way
Suite 202
Nashville, TN 37228-9940
615-736-5820

Newark Area Office
1 Newark Center
21st Floor
Newark, NJ 07102-5233
973-645-6383

New Orleans District Office
701 Loyola Avenue
Suite 600
New Orleans, LA 70113-9936
504-589-2329

New York District Office
33 Whitehall St.
11th Floor
New York, NY 10004
212-336-3620

Norfolk Area Office
Federal Building
200 Granby Street
Suite 739
Norfolk, VA 23510
757-441-3470

Oakland Local Office
1301 Clay Street
Suite 1170-N
Oakland, CA 94612-5217
510-637-3230

Oklahoma Area Office
210 Park Avenue
Oklahoma City, OK 73102
405-231-4911

Philadelphia District Office
21 South 5th Street
4th Floor
Philadelphia, PA 19106
215-440-2600

Phoenix District Office
3300 North Central Avenue
Suite 690
Phoenix, AZ 85012-2504
602-640-5000

Pittsburgh Area Office
1001 Liberty Avenue
Suite 300
Pittsburgh, PA 15222-4187
412-644-3444

Raleigh Area Office
1309 Annapolis Drive
Raleigh, NC 27608-2129
919-856-4064

Richmond Area Office
830 East Main Street
Suite 600
Richmond, VA 23219
804-771-2200

San Antonio District Office
Mockingbird Plaza II
5410 Fredericksburg Road
Suite 200
San Antonio, TX 78229-3555
210-281-7600

San Diego Area Office
401 B Street
Suite 510
San Diego, CA 92101
619-557-7235

San Francisco District Office
350 The Embarcadero
Suite 500
San Francisco, CA 94105-1260
415-625-5600

San Jose Local Office
96 North 3rd Street
Suite 200
San Jose, CA 95112
408-291-7352

San Juan Area Office
525 F.D. Roosevelt Avenue
Plaza Las Americas
Suite 1202
San Juan, Puerto Rico 00918-8001
787-771-1464

Savannah Local Office
410 Mall Boulevard
Suite G
Savannah, GA 31406-4821
912-652-4234

Seattle District Office
Federal Office Building
909 First Avenue
Suite 400
Seattle, WA 98104-1061
206-220-6883

St. Louis District Office
Robert A. Young Building
1222 Spruce Street
Room 8.100
St. Louis, MO 63103
314-539-7800

Tampa Area Office
501 East Polk Street
10th Floor
Tampa, FL 33602
813-228-2310

Washington Field Office
1801 L Street, N.W.
Suite 100
Washington, D.C. 20507
202-419-0713

Appendix F

Miscellaneous State Laws of Interest

This appendix contains various state laws of interest to individuals facing a termination.

ARIZONA—By statute: employer commits wrongful discharge if it terminates employee in violation of written contract or statute, in retaliation for refusal of employee to commit illegal act, for reasonably reporting illegal acts of employer, or because employee has exercised certain constitutional or statutory rights.

Constructive discharge is limited to specific conditions.

CONNECTICUT—Prohibits discharge of employee by public or private employer for exercising free speech rights set forth in the United States and Connecticut constitutions provided employee speaks out for matter of public, not private, concern, and such activity does not substantially interfere with the employee's bona fide performance or the working relationship between the employee and the employer.

DELAWARE—Employees have right to inspect personnel files and take notes, but not obtain copy of file.

INDIANA—Upon termination, if requested, employer must give "service letter," setting forth the nature and character of the service rendered by the employee, the duration thereof, and "truly states" the cause the employee quit or was discharged, unless it does not require written recommendation or application showing qualifications or experience when hiring.

If employer contracts in writing to make payments to an employee benefit plan it must give written notice of its failure to do so. Employees may recover double damages from employer who fails to give notice and make payment.

KENTUCKY—Prohibits employer from requiring employees to arbitrate employment claims.

MAINE—Upon written demand, employer must state reasons for termination in writing within fifteen days of written request.

Severance pay statutorily mandated for industrial or commercial employers of one-hundred or more employees, if relocate one-hundred miles or more distance or terminate business, equal to one week of pay per year of service.

MASSACHUSETTS—Group life insurance coverage must continue for 31 days following termination of employment.

Employees must be notified of conversion rights if any.

In the event of insolvency of NMO enrolled individuals may enroll with any NMO available during enrollee's last enrollment period.

Enrollees to be offered same coverage and rates as available during last enrollment period.

Employees may inspect and copy personnel file.

MINNESOTA—Unlawful to persuade workers to change their employment by knowingly false representation.

If requested in writing within fifteen working days of termination, employer must give written statement to employee of truthful reason for termination within ten working days of request.

Statement may not be made the subject of a legal action for defamation.

Employee may inspect and copy personnel files.

MISSOURI—Employer having seven or more employees must provide employee who has worked at least ninety days and is discharged or quits, upon written request, with specific reference to the statute, by certified mail within one year, a letter signed by a manager or superintendent setting forth the nature and character of service rendered and duration thereof, and truly stating for what cause the employee was discharged or quit service.

MONTANA—Common law wrongful discharge eliminated. After probationary period, and if no other period is established, six months, discharge is wrongful if not for good cause, or if in retaliation for employee's refusal to violate public policy, or for reporting violation of public policy, or where employer violated express provisions of its own personnel policy. Employee may recover punitive damages if proves by clear and convincing evidence the employer committed fraud or engaged in actual malice when terminating employee.

NEVADA—An employee may not be disciplined or discharged on information of a special agent, detective or "spotter," in a matter involving question of integrity or honesty, or violation of rules, without a hearing, and an opportunity to face the accuser and furnish testimony in defense.

NEW YORK—Employer must notify terminated employee in writing of dates of termination and cancellation of employee benefits within 5 days of termination.

Covered employees contribute $\frac{1}{2}$ of 1% of wages, not to exceed 60¢ per week, and covered employer to provide remainder of cost for disability benefits for up to 26 weeks for non-occupational injury or sickness.

RHODE ISLAND—For employers of fifty or more, a severance payment to employees employed at least three years of two weeks' pay for every year of service if terminated within twelve months in some cases and twenty-four months in others, after a change in control of the company.

VERMONT—Certain employers must reinstate disabled workers if recovery occurs within two years.

WASHINGTON—Employees may inspect their personnel file at least annually.

Appendix G

Notable Wrongful Discharge Cases

The public policy tort of wrongful discharge has been recognized in most—but not all—states over the past twenty-five years. The following is a list of some of the more notable cases from around the country that have fostered its development and illustrate its scope.

ALABAMA

Overton v. Amerex Corp., 642 So.2d 450 (Ala. 1994) (for seeking workers' compensation) (where cause of action created by statute).

Refusal to expand tort to other cases expressed in Wright v. Dothan, Chrysler, Plymouth, Dodge, Inc., 658 So.2d 428 (Ala. 1995).

ARIZONA

Wagenseller v. Scottsdale Memorial Hospital, 710 P.2d 1025 (Ariz. 1985) (for refusal to engage in mooning).

Vermillion v. AAA Pro Moving & Storage, 704 P.2d 1360 (Ariz. 1985) (for reporting theft by his employer).

Murcott v. Best Western, Int'l, 9 P.3d 1088 (Ariz. 2000) (for complaining internally about possible antitrust violations).

ARKANSAS

Webb v. HCA Health Servs, 780 S.W.2d 571 (Ark. 1989) (for a hospital employee's refusal to falsify patient records).

Sterling Drug, Inc. v. Oxford, 743 S.W.2d 380 (Ark. 1998) (for reporting employer submitted false information to government—but contract damages only).

CALIFORNIA

Petermann v. Int'l Brotherhood of Teamsters, Local 396, 344 P.2d 25 (Cal. 1959 (for refusing to commit perjury).

Tameny v. Atlantic Richfield Co., 610 P.2d 1330 (Cal. 1980) (for refusing to participate in illegal price fixing).

Stevenson v. Superior Court, 16 Cal.4th 880 (1997) (for discharge contrary to public policy expressed in state age discrimination statute).

Grant-Burton v. Covenant Care, Inc., 99 Cal.App.4th 1361 (2002) (for discussing wages, where such discussions were protected by statute).

COLORADO

Martin Marrieta Corp. v. Lorenz, 823 P.2d 100 (Colo. 1992) (for refusal to misrepresent quality control deficiencies and unrealistic cost assessments to government).

Rocky Mountain Hosp. v. Mariani, 916 P.2d 519 (Colo. 1996) (for refusing to falsify accounting information).

CONNECTICUT

Sheets v. Teddy's Frosted Foods, Inc., 427 A.2d 385 (Conn. 1980) (for reporting food labeling irregularities).

Lewis v. Nationwide Mut. Ins. Co., 19 IER 1470 (D. Conn. 2003) (for demonstrating loyalty to company insureds as required by Rules of Professional Conduct).

DELAWARE

Heller v. Dover Warehouse Market, Inc., 515 A.2d 178 (Del. 1986) (on basis of reports of unlawful polygraph).

Schuster v. Derocili, 775 A.2d 1029 (Del. 2001) (discharge contrary to public policy against sexual harassment expressed in state's discrimination statute).

DISTRICT OF COLUMBIA

Adams v. George W. Chochran & Co., Inc., 597 A.2d 28 (DC Ct. App. 1991) (for refusal to drive a truck without a required inspection sticker).

HAWAII

Parnar v. Americana Hotels, 652 P.2d 625 (Haw. 1982) (for reporting potential antitrust violations to a company attorney).

Smith v. Chaney Brooks Realty, 865 P.2d 170 (Haw. 1994) (for inquiring about the propriety of certain paycheck deductions).

IDAHO

Jackson v. Minidoka Irr. Dist., 563 P.2d 54 (Id. 1977) (must violate public policy).

Ray v. Nampa School Dist. No. 131, 814 P.2d 17 (Id. 1991) (for reporting electrical and building codes violations).

Hummer v. Evans, 923 P.2d 981 (Id. 1996) (for complying with court-issued subpoena).

Crea v. FMC Corp., 16 P.3d 272 (Id. 2000) (for disclosing employer's responsibility for arsenic contamination of groundwater).

ILLINOIS

Palmateer v. International Harvester Co., 421 N.E.2d 876 (Ill. 1981) (for reporting the crime of a co-worker).

Hinthorn v. Roland's of Bloomington, Inc., 519 N.E.2d 909 (Ill. 1988) (for seeking medical attention associated with work-related injury).

Pietruszynski v. The McClier Corp., 788 N.E.2d 82 (Ill. 2003) (for testifying or expressing intent to testify in workers' compensation proceedings).

INDIANA

Frampton v. Central Indiana Gas Co., 297 N.E.2d 425 (Ind. 1973) (for filing workers' compensation claim).

McClanahan v. Remington Freight Lines, Inc., 517 N.E.2d 390 (Ind. 1988) (for refusing to drive an overweight truck in violation of law).

IOWA

Woodruff v. Associated Grocers of Iowa, Inc., 364 N.W.2d 215 (Iowa 1985) (for reporting that employer was keeping two sets of accounting books).

Springer v. Weeks & Leo Co., Inc., 429 N.W.2d 558 (Iowa 1988) (for filing workers' compensation claim).

Fitzgerald v. Salsbury Chemical, Inc., 613 N.W.2d 275 (Iowa 2000) (for providing truthful testimony in co-workers discrimination case).

KANSAS

Palmer v. Brown, 752 P.2d 685 (Kan. 1988) (for reporting Medicaid fraud).

KENTUCKY

Firestone Textile Co. Div. Firestone Tire & Rubber Co. v. Meadows, 666 S.W.2d 730 (Ky. 1983) (for pursuing workers' compensation claim).

Brown v. Physician's Mut. Ins. Co., 679 S.W.2d 836 (Ky. App. 1984) (for attempting to report procedural irregularities to outside agency).

Northeast Health Management Inc. v. Cotton, 56 S.W.3d 440 (Ky.Ct.App. 2001) (constructively discharged for refusal to commit perjury on behalf of supervisor).

LOUISIANA

Bartlett v. Reese, 569 So.2d 195 (La. Ct. App. 1990) (for reporting possible environmental violations by third party to state agency).

Cahill v. Frank's Door & Building Supply Co., Inc., 590 So.2d 53 (La. 1991) (for filing workers' compensation claim).

MARYLAND

Kessler v. Equity Management, Inc., 572 A.2d 1144 (Md. 1990) (refusal to conduct unlawful search).

MASSACHUSETTS

Flesnor v. Technical Communications Corp., 575 N.E.2d 1107 (Mass. 1991) (constructively discharged for cooperating with customs service criminal investigation of employer's exporting activities).

MICHIGAN

Sventko v. Kroger Co., 245 N.W.2d 151 (Mich. 1976) (for filing workers' compensation claim).

Trombetta v. Detroit, Toledo & Fronton R. Co., 265 N.W.2d 385 (Mich. 1978) (for refusing to alter pollution reports).

Watassek v. Michigan Dept. of Mental Health, 372 N.W.2d 617 (Mich. 1985) (for reporting patient abuse).

Garavaglia v. Centro, Inc., 536 N.W.2d 805 (Mich.Ct.App. 1995) (discharged as employer's bargaining representative due to union pressure).

MINNESOTA

Phipps v. Clark Oil & Refining Corp., 408 N.W.2d 569 (Minn. 1987) (for refusal to pump leaded gasoline into vehicle designed for unleaded gasoline).

Clough v. Ertz, 442 N.W.2d 798 (Minn.Ct.App. 1989) (for reporting to county attorney mayor's request DWI laws not be enforced).

MISSISSIPPI

McArn v. Allied Bruce—Terminex Co., 626 So.2d 603 (Miss. 1993) (for refusing to defraud a customer).

Drake v. Advance Constr. Serv., 117 F.3d 203 (5th Cir. 1997) (interpreting Mississippi law) (for refusing to conceal deficiencies in employer's government contract performance).

MISSOURI

Kirk v. Mercy Hospital Tri-County, 851 S.W.2d 617 (Mo. App. 1993) (for refusal by nurse to *stay out of it* in case of questionable patient care).

Saffels v. Rice, 40 F.3d 1546 (8th Cir. 1994) (interpreting Missouri law) (discharge due to employer's mistaken belief employee had reported FLSA violations to authorities).

NEBRASKA

Ambroz v. Conrhuskers Square Ltd., 416 N.W.2d 510 (Neb. 1987) (for refusing to take unlawful polygraph examination).

Jackson v. Morris Communications Corp., 657 N.W.2d 634 (Neb. 2003) (for exercising workers' compensation rights).

NEVADA

Hansen v. Harrah's, 675 P.2d 394 (Nev. 1984) (for filing workers' compensation claim).

D'Angelo v. Gardner, 819 P.2d 206 (Nev. 1991) (for refusal to work in an unsafe and unhealthful work environment).

NEW HAMPSHIRE

Cloutier v. Great Atlantic & Pacific Tea Co., Inc., 436 A.2d 1140 (N.H. 1981) (for attempting to comply with OSHA statute in maintaining safe workplace).

NEW JERSEY

Pierce v. Ortho Pharmaceutical Corp., 417 A.2d 505 (N.J. 1980) (for doctor refusing to violate Hippocratic Oath).

Lally v. Copygraphics, 428 A.2d 1317 (N.J. 1981) (for filing workers' compensation claim).

MacDougall v. Weichert, 677 A.2d 162 (N.J. 1996) (for casting vote on town council opposed by employer's client).

NEW MEXICO

Chavez v. Manville Products Corp., 777 P.2d 371 (N.M. 1989) (for opposing unauthorized use of employee's names in employer's lobbying efforts).

NEW YORK

Weider v. Skala, 609 N.E.2d 105 (N.Y. 1992) (refusal to violate professional ethics code).

NORTH CAROLINA

Coman v. Thomas Mfg. Co. Inc., 381 S.E.2d 445 (N.C. 1989) (for refusing to falsify records and drive truck in violation of federal law).

Deerman v. Beverly Cal. Corp., 518 S.E.2d 804 (N.C. 1999) (for fulfilling statutory duties as nurse in providing advice to family of patient to change physicians).

NORTH DAKOTA

Krein v. Marian Manor Nursing Home, 415 N.W.2d 793 (N.D. 1987) (for seeking workers' compensation benefits).

Resler v. Humane Soc'y, 480 N.W.2d 429 (N.D. 1992) (for giving truthful testimony pursuant to subpoena).

OHIO

Greeley v. Miami Valley Maintenance Contractors, Inc., 551 N.E.2d 981 (Ohio 1990) (for having wages assigned to satisfy support obligations).

Celeste v. Wiseco Piston, 784 N.E.2d 1198 (Ohio 2003) (for expressing concerns to management about safety of company's products).

OKLAHOMA

Burk v. K-Mart Corp., 770 P.2d 24 (Okla. 1989) (must be contrary to clear mandate of public policy in constitutional, statutory or decisional law).

McGehee v. Florafax Int'l, Inc., 776 P.2d 852 (Okla. 1989) (for refusing to commit perjury).

Sargent v. Central Nat'l Bank & Trust Co., 809 P.2d 1298 (Okla. 1991) (for refusing to alter report to audit committee).

OREGON

Nees v. Hocks, 536 P.2d 512 (Or. 1975) (for reporting to jury duty).

Delaney v. Taco Time Int'l, Inc., 681 P.2d 114 (Or. 1984) (for refusing to defame a co-worker).

PENNSYLVANIA

Raykovitz v. K-Mart Corp., 665 A.2d 833 (Pa.Super.Ct. 1995) (where part-time employee who had lost full-time position was discharged for seeking to collect unemployment compensation for loss of full-time work).

Shick v. Shirey, 716 A.2d 1231 (Penn. 1998) (for filing workers' compensation benefits).

Rothrock v. Rothrock Motor Sales, Inc., 810 A.2d 114 (Pa.Super. 2002) (for refusing to dissuade subordinate from filing workers' compensation claim).

SOUTH CAROLINA

Ludwick v. This Minute of Carolina, Inc., 337 S.E.2d 213 (S.C. 1985) (for honoring subpoena).

Garner v. Morrison Knuden Corp., 456 S.E.2d 907 (S.C. 1995) (for reporting and testifying about radioactive contamination and unsafe working conditions at nuclear facility).

SOUTH DAKOTA

Johnson v. Kreiser's, Inc., 433 N.W.2d 225 (S.D. 1988) (for refusing to commit unlawful act).

Dahl v. Combined Ins. Co., 621 N.W.2d 163 (S.D. 2001) (for reporting missing insurance premiums to regulators).

TENNESSEE

Clanton v. Cain-Sloan Co., 677 S.W.2d 441 (Tenn. 1984) (for exercise of workers' compensation rights).

Hodges v. S.C. Toof & Co., 833 S.W.2d 896 (Tenn. 1992) (for performing jury service).

Crews v. Buckman Labs Int'l, Inc., 78 S.W.3d 852 (Tenn. 2002) (for reporting the employer's general counsel did not possess a Tennessee license to practice law).

TEXAS

Sabine Pitot Service, Inc. v. Hauke, 687 S.W.2d 733 (Tex. 1985) (for refusal to illegally pump ship's bilges into coastal waters prohibited by federal law).

Ed Rachal Foundation v. D'Unger, 117 S.W.3d 348 (Tex.Ct.App. 2003) (for disobeying instructions to ignore mistreatment of transient trespassers).

UTAH

Peterson v. Browning, 832 P.2d 1280 (Utah 1992) (for refusing to falsify documents in violation of law).

Heslop v. Bank of Utah, 839 P.2d 828 (Utah 1992) (for objecting to false reporting of bank's income and assets contrary to law).

Spratley v. State Farm Mut. Auto Ins. Co., 78 P.3d 603 (Utah 2003) (lawyer constructively discharged by requirement to violate ethical rules).

VERMONT

Payne v. Rozendaal, 520 A.2d 586 (Vt. 1986) (discriminatory discharge on basis of age stated cause of action under public policy exception).

VIRGINIA

Bowman v. State Bank of Keysville, 331 S.E.2d 797 (Va. 1985) (for refusing to succumb to duress to vote shares of stock in a way favorable to employer).

Lockhart v. Commonwealth Educ. Sys. Corp., 439 S.E.2d 328 (Va. 1994) (tort claim of alleged discriminatory discharge based on race and gender).

WASHINGTON

Thompson v. St. Regis Paper Co., 685 P.2d 1081 (Wash. 1984) (for attempting to bring company in compliance with Foreign Corrupt Practices Act).

Gardner v. Loomis Armored, 913 P.2d 377 (Wash. 1996) (for leaving truck unattended to help rescue hostages who were being threatened by a man with a knife).

Hubbard v. Spokane Co., 50 P.3d 602 (Wash. 2002) (over difference of opinion concerning the legality of issuing a hotel building permit).

WEST VIRGINIA

Harless v. First Nat'l Bank in Fairmont, 246 S.E.2d 270 (W.Va. 1978) (for telling superiors at a bank customers were being mischarged on installment loans).

Lilly v. Overnight Transp. Co., 425 S.E.2d 214 (W.Va. 1992) (for refusing to operate a vehicle with brakes so unsafe as to create a danger to the public).

Kanagy v. Fiesta Salons, Inc., 541 S.E.2d 616 (W.Va. 2000) (for providing information to regulatory board about use of unlicensed personnel).

WISCONSIN

Kempfer v. Automotive Finishing, Inc., 564 N.W.2d 692 (Wis. 1997) (for refusing to drive a truck because he lacked a valid commercial driver's license).

Strozinsky v. School District of Brown Deer, 614 N.W.2d 443 (Wis. 2000) (for complying with federal income tax withholding laws).

WYOMING

Griess v. Consolidated Freightways Corp. of Delaware, 776 P.2d 752 (Wyo. 1989) (for filing a workers' compensation claim).

Index

ABOUT THE AUTHOR

Richard C. Busse obtained his law degree in 1974 from the University of California, Hastings College of the Law. He began practicing employment law in 1975. From 1975 to 1981, he defended employment cases, both with a defense firm and in his capacity as Chief Deputy County Counsel for Multnomah County, Oregon—the state's most populous county.

In 1981, he set out on his own to develop a plaintiff's employment litigation practice, and has practiced in that field ever since. He is now senior partner in the Portland law firm of Busse & Hunt, which is devoted exclusively to the practice of plaintiff's employment law. Mr. Busse represents victims of wrongful discharge, discrimination, defamation, and other workplace torts. His cases have established important legal precedents in the field. He is a frequent speaker and has published articles on employment law since 1981. Mr. Busse is also the author of the best-selling *Employees' Rights: Your Practical Handbook To Workplace Law,* Sphinx Publishing (2004).

Mr. Busse has been listed in the national peer review publication *The Best Lawyers in America* every year since 1989 for labor and employment law in Oregon. His firm was named the leading plaintiff's employment law firm in Oregon by Chambers US, America's Leading Business Lawyers, 2003-04; and he was awarded its highest individual rating. The nationally known legal directory, *Martindale-Hubbell*, also gives Mr. Busse and his firm its highest rating for legal ability and ethics.